Blue Jesus

Rick Watson

High Plains Creole Press
Coyote LoFI Productions
© 2014 Rick Watson

Cover design by Dustin Hansen
platypusman.com

ISBN 978-0-9899677-2-3

Once again on the edge of December on these darkling plains, thanks to the kindness of Paul Yellow Bird (secrets) a book is done, a book is born—

Some of this is as old as 1966—it was written, spoken and dreamed and then written and edited—edited mostly by Paul.

I thank him with all love, and any wasted words are mine.

Advent/Christmas, 2014

TABLE OF CONTENTS

Part I: A Briefly Noted Eternity

Read Proverbs 8. Whoever she may be, this book is dedicated to her…
And to Minot State, to Jonelle Watson and to Helen Watson, who put their lives into that place of Higher Learning

My friend sends a note that autocorrected "Fest" to read as "Fear"—

I was sitting outside meditating, mostly worrying, and this very weathered looking robin was acting odd. I started talking to it, and it began doing its odd behavior closer and closer. I said, "You're pretty close to me, but you must know you could still get away if I jumped." I went back to what I was doing, and after a bit I heard flapping, then chirp-chirp really close. I looked down and it was close to me on my chair, so close that it was sitting mostly on my clothing. I stayed very calm so as not to disturb it, spoke to it asking if it wanted me to help it somehow. After about a minute it flopped down and sat on my foot. Just as I was wondering if it had something wrong with it, it flew away.

Wonder what kind of medicine this is. Does this happen a lot to people who sit in their backyards?
—Jesse Watson

A poem happened to you—
Here is one from the book of Kells,
A song I set back to music—
"The trees like a hedge surround me
The black bird sings to me..."

It is called "The Irish Monks Song", a gloss a Monk inserted into the book. I worked from three versions of the English Translation and wrote my own music—you

actually got to be the monk with a robin, much more fun
than black birds or cuckoos—I think it does happen to
some people—obviously, I would tell you that you had a
visit from the Holy Spirit, or Sister Wisdom. Does it
happen to a lot of people? No, because they do not sit
still—I work with many people who never sit still—God
has to chase them.
Just the other day, God said,
"You humans are so hard to catch"—
I said, "Free Will?"
And God said, "No; Cars, computers, telephones,
twaddle, twitter or taps…"

1

Sit beside the lake
Look into the water
Look at the stones beneath the water
What is beneath the stones?
Listen to the thunder
Stare into the rolling clouds
Watch the turtle a few feet away
Imitate the turtle
In what clear way
Do humans and animals differ?
Animals try not to make
The same error twice

***

The question is asked, often:
Why do so many Christians know so little about their
    book?
There is, I suppose, little excuse today.
Christians are "literate", and the Bible is everywhere,

Available in more painstaking translations
And in more reader friendly versions than there were
    tongues at Pentecost.
"Oh we been doin' that under the awning strut,
Breakin' our own legs!
Leave them expectant advent candles lit;
Attract fire moths on the 4th of July—
Freedom burns, wings fry, Messiah's journey,
    incomplete—
Time lines, I told you twice, are lies of circles, points and
    angles—
The compass rose is red with God's own blood, a crown
    of thorns—
God rides on a parabolic curve—

2

The sand runs soap and opera through the hourglass

It is clogged with one tough grain of sand in its tiny
    pinched-in waist—
The sundial fakes eternal now—sun and solid earth will
    melt
Under the cedar's solid shade; these are lines, the lies
    we made
In heat and hot head anger, slow motion, blue electronic
    fires—
We used an auger, screw lifted wheat up in the silver sun
    shot
Grain bins there in a cloud of motion made from harvest
    dust—

3

"Time to Steal Time"

Dust clouds under those northern sun downs, powdered
August—Up the grain spiraled, drifted, danced against all
gravity could hold back—(from waste and time)—each
kernel of grain held a space between each gasp for air and
grace—(eternity means love)—to slip against the pull of
earth, break free, make memory, hope like bread—Here is
the list of the exiles we managed to save:
I embrace this mental, back-spacing mediation of
memory task with my eyelids peeled against the light of
God; I never blink, not once—tears and revelations
sought; memory was, is, all of this—let's meet the
martyrs, safely dead and saved—Look with me at this
epic inner outer vision here!

&&&

On the last day of summer to decide just what we were
     after,
8 am, some Christmas lights? The fog lifts curtains
     against white sky,
Trees and sidewalks, lawns, and Empty Street—
Just enough of the scent of rain to let me know the snow,
     and skipping down the tail of the year we go—
Let us list and memorize the saved:
First let's meet where words make eyes,
More melody than meaning or just mean—
We'll face the end by saying things are better

Instead of sneakily getting worse—
There's the morning's fried fish smell left from the night
     before,

5

While down the hall in the bathroom, it's all silken ears
    and sweet sow's purse—

Were God and Einstein both dyslectic,
Or is it us, my cousins with no tail?
You'd have to know which universe we're in—
Science doesn't know, and the Bible doesn't mind or
    care—

4

But allow us: remember the sons with the M1 Carbines

Through the wasteland that was Europe,
The waste of the great late West,
Blood and concrete, shrapnel, rubber,
Rations stamped with chaos codes, "K" and "C"
And then some bowels, body parts, more blood,
Bombed-out, mortared forests,
Mountains, hills and holy cities,
Heretical, historical, holy crippled dreams—
Metallic angel fire from metal wings
In the Celtic-Germanic skies—
But how should we remember?
Oh, yes, Veterans Day—
Terror, sorrow, make for
Courage, woman, child and man—
Terror, discipline burned by death
And fire into human grace,
Which came that night, after the fire,
A chill, a real evening breeze—
"A soldier is more alive, awake,
To terror and wonder in the fields of death

Than he will ever be again," the one legged old man says:
Rex of the jug of brandy captured, and
Escaped, with the General in his Jeep,
Barron who ran when he could not crawl
And dodged the strafing planes,
The guy from Nebraska who went back
Home to the meat packing plant and "was never
Bothered by the smell of butchered pigs again,"
Kalippa, Hawaiian Sarge from hell who fished
For supper with a hand grenade,
And Henry who came home to engender me;
He bounced the bullets off his eye balls,
And caught mortar shells in his teeth from the Bulge to
    the Philippines—
Time to steal the time my boys, after they say the War is
    done.

5

Two white clouds that look like interlocked smoke rings
Circle about the absolute stillness, green trees—
Then the noise of people, live music,
A pure pearl white half-moon
Slips across the kind of blue sky
That comes only after the August storms
Or Canadian northwesters
A few weeks before September goes

Two mourning doves duet when the music is done—
One old buzzard soars and seeks dead meat
Above the shelter belts to the east—
A big flock of white water birds, on their way nowhere,
Not migrating or eating bugs on the wing—
They seem to be aerial designers

In the rosy space between the earth and moon—

Excursus—

Christians don't read the Bible—they hear the Bible read.
There is a difference.
And if Christians are not regular participants
Where the Bible is read extensively,
They do not read.

Also, Preachers: do you preach on the text?

Or is the teXt a pretext?
Literally how many words from that appointed text for
    the day?
How many phrases do you quote?
How many are paraphrased, how many summarized?
Here is a check:
If your listener remembers your illustrations
And does not remember the text you preached,
You are in trouble.
A group of young folks are having a Meyers-Briggs
    Personality Inventory Party.
What if they had a shindig and read aloud from the book
    of Proverbs instead?

6

Grandfather Mountain

Guess a short grass boy should learn some things
Before he strolls in the Blue Ridge—
I am amazed—the top of my head was burned
By the power of the sun

On a foggy rainy morning
On the top of Grand Father Mountain
Always carry a cap—
The oldest mountains
Have some holy lessons to teach—
I looked down from the hanging bridge
And learned the difference between
A mile horizontal
And a mile vertical, for sure,
And as I looked across the ridges
I learned another shade of blues
While a turkey buzzard
Even higher still
Kept saying, "Ha! Ha! Ha!"

7

Eyes ahead on the long southern shadows of the solstice
    afternoon—
Sunlight bursts through the big window into the bones of
    my face—
So close my eyes—sun wheels pin wheel in a violent
    circle—
Violet, purple, and red, then the wind creaks the wooden
    beams
Of the roof and I sing along inside—
Lay me down, burnt bones,
Toasted flesh, cremated, powdered mistakes
On a southern slope of hill where the sun comes daily,
Stronger each day, the covered ashes repent and are ripe
    for Redux—
Gumbo and grass roots linger right above, so my ashes
Can hear the wind blow in the grass
That will last until the word is spoken again,

And the light bursts in to raise our lives together—
New heaven, New earth, same old hill—

There's joy and grief on either side of the simple face—
That we die of old age while making our future plans—
I plan to pray for a simpler plan
That would activate all the imaginations
In Dawkins, St John, Hitchens and Lucifer's minds—
Trapped in the fossil called evolution,
The slipknot noose of DNA toots like a fart!

8

The woman of business needs a plan to help,
As she grandly salutes and shoots at me:
"I can't help it if they can't afford a home;
It's the law of Supply and Demand."
I pray as she turns slowly in the wind
On her cross of profit and loss—
May her multiverse unfold in love—
May she say and be the one to make it truth:
"My business is charity, faith and hope"
Now, rear-guarding God—
Apple tree, snow
White on black
Eve in the feathers of a friendly crow

9

The Cherry Tree Carol?
Sing it again.
Calling God by another name
Might induce the deaf to hear the tune—

Snow this morning, another inch—
That strange and beautiful silence on Sunday,
No breeze in the early grey-white sky—
Smoke straight up from the chimneys—
Then a perfect lilac over the lights
Of the valley below while the light on the
Street, balcony, drive ways,
Holds on to electric green and blue—

10

Steal Time

It was 60 degrees according to the new sign on Broadway,
On the 5th of January I say,
He says, "I looked for some snow, no snow—
Some ice, big wind, real dust,
Water puddles but not a bit of snow"—
It makes me feel dislocated, I say—

Right, he says, and then,
He says, "I saw a red and green ribbon,
Some kind of left over wrap on
The dead grass out front of the house—"
"Left over Christmas," I say,
"Abandoned decorations
Some soldier threw away," he says—

I wonder; do we know what he means?
WW2 is still his home, and we are often

Ghosts to him, we are so very far away—

The flock of small winter birds
Looks like a leaf pile
Tossed up and flung against
The wind, hard, that Northwest Wind—
They make black dots and
Pencil strokes again the sky: you stare—

I saw an M1 carbine in a museum with
Black marks just like those birds—
Once they clutched, grasped, clung to
The firmament of stock against cheek bone,
Eyes squinted down sights way too many times—
The time stands still, and they feel the wood
Against their skin and fingers 60 years on—
The sun glares in the wide windows of the room—
Close your eyes and sleep for a bit—
You will wake in the night and not remember the
    dreams—
This is all about the resonance of
A trumpet blast across the air of a graveyard
Under the ancient blue of memorial sky
Against the crack of an old Springfield,
A newer M1 or even an M16—
The snap of flags,
The distant sound of a tractor in a feed pen,
Like clanking treads—It fades,
That reverberation across the stones

Roosevelt, Stalin and Churchill,
Pearl Harbor, Dunkirk, Leningrad, Auschwitz, and
    Bataan,
Normandy, Bulge, to Hiroshima,
Mad whoop and roar of victory parades!

What do you know, kid? Vietnam?

I doubt it—just lists of names—
Now Iraq, Iran, Alphaganistanagain,
Where you weren't on 9/11—
The towers came down when he was over 80—
He told me then: "Now we get to see how
America does when the blood is on our land."—
He was 92 last December—he remembers
Hobnail boots on a hard wood floor,
A spike through the head as you waded ashore
Quick now, he'll tell you,
How many dead men still swim for shore,
Died on the beachheads, crumbled and stumbled,
And not what their names were,
But what were the names of the beaches?
All of them, all, that's all he remembers now—

Time to steal away from time, these brief eternal words:
Barely to bed and my legs go wild enough to
Run me through a wake, a war and a hunt
Like the vexed and nightmare-ridden dog I am—
Then I dream my dead wife is here—

At 5 am I get up and lean against the wall
To doze and dance with the demons there,
All of me like the old V8's in old Detroit,
Like a shell-shocked vet in the Windsor ditch,
The cure for all the bad dreams you can have—
I wake up, survive the wars again, alive—
But today by middle afternoon the temps drop down—
The fog rolls thick and there's fire in my stove,
And faces float across the empty room—
I put up the screen and sleep the sleep
An old man sleeps when a few bad nights
Have made their way with sorrow in his bones,
His sins, and big death's final pricks—

11

The near full moon, once again,
Set in the west so bright at dawn,
Just like the first and last day come at once,
A trick of light and
A slip of earth to moon and sun, and gone,
Here in the middle of the middle lands,
And the chance to know its meaning
Wasn't lost on me this time—

What's it mean? What's mean?
Pay attention kids and English Profs—
Make a note and write this down—
You can see when your eyes are closed—

If we could tell you what it meant
It wouldn't be a poem—
It would be a formula—

In a holy place
You carry place
In a sacred time

What this country needs, is god, she said—
What we have is gods, I say to her—
What we need is what God does—

12

Love, you move
Still as a shadow at desire's speed—

I can't catch up
While I am at rest; slow down—
Sit still with me and we make love
With God at the speed of light—

13

Rip off your face to hide your nose—
Go naked so no one can see
Your old clothes in the dark—
Save your hammer and your nails—
The cross is a place for morning—
Your cross is a place for mourning—
"Free associate," he says to me,
"That's all you do."—
I say, "Association's never free—
It costs so much; it's not for sale—
It creates a responsibility, you see?
Accountability, time traps, free?"

At my funeral if you say:
"He preached; he taught;
A statesman too; a minister;
Liberality was his to give." I'll say,
"Sit down and shut yer mouth:
Hot head, big-mouth Cracked pot profiteer,
A quitter dreamer poet
Of too many stories,
And a minstrel of the
Songs that no one sings, I say,
Shut yer mouth; you told the truth—

"Or, she loved him there right to his end,
And his sons all came back home—

Their wives all thought him a sweet old guy
And grandkids wept real tears, OK—"

But mostly traps, associations
Are prison words to cover dust
And ignore pure blinding lights
Which will rise one day and then return,
Complete—you and me and every
Sorry strand of DNA and memory verse,
Each atomic angel star dust legend
And we will, in our mighty host, say,
Oh, so that is God?

14

Sit in the arm chair—
First light takes on sun heat,
And, your eyes, half shut,
Not asleep or a cat nap, but
A dose of silent truth,
Float on the chair in the
Fluid flesh of old dry bone—
A moment's wisdom,
And you know that the city
Gates where Wisdom waits
Are right behind your eyes—
The sweet sensation of her fur,
Her female loved one's fur,
Runs orange and gold on
Tiger feet for the length of
Your long roads in your blood:
Not indolence, or ignorance,
But incarnate, ecstatic joy—
Drift in God outside your mind:

Steal time and be redeemed—

15

And A Fool Who Sings

The same old Pheasant Cock,
Pompous strut and statesman's walk,
Steps out blazing in the street,
Checks the progress on the
House that's going up next to his hill,
Comes across, inspects my lawn,
Ignores me, glares and then is gone—

The blue jay screams out in the tree,
Blazed bright blue flag on a branch,
Takes his tax in peanut pay,
Screams once more, flies away,
And shouts from shadows in the trees
Like some obsessive maddened thing,
And now this street has three odd kings:
Pheasant, Jay and a fool who sings—

Excursus—

Doc Watson, the man who taught American roots music
with one guitar and a few friends from the Deep Hollow,
North Carolina for over 50 years, with no eyes to see the
strings, died near the spot in the Blue Ridge where he was
born and lived. He got a few lines in Rolling Stone.
Charlie Sheen, the suicidal,
Flat Screen freak wants to extend his 15
Minutes of bad publicity

And lands a cover and an interview in the issue of that
date.
Anyone have trouble hearing what is going, going...
gone?

16

For As Long As The Wind Played The Song

Sit in this chair here, by the open door—
Listen to the sirens,
The honk, hum and engine gun,
The train whistle rail bang

From half a block down the hill—
You will hear the wind
Play tunes in the woods—
Morning light hits
Leaves in the most familiar
Impossible flick of
Yellow green: sparkle so
Monet could paint it a thousand
Times and still not get it right,
And no one could record that song—

What would be so wrong with you
If you sat right in that chair
And listened to the Cottonwoods
For as long as the wind took time to play the tune?

17

Across The West Above A Storm

It was a dream
Deep in the streets of a town
Made of stone so old
The gray of its surface shined in light,
And at my feet the
Bricks were grooved
From carriage wheels,
Dug by hooves,
And worn by feet—

I knew the one who showed
Me all around the place,
The church, a dance hall,
A huge room full
Of great wooden tables,
With paintings on the walls—
I had no name to speak—

I woke up as I stood in the street,
Wild with the knowledge that
Some things last a long, wide time,
Looked out the window to the valley below
One year after the mythic flood,
And still so many stones to go—
Why not admit it? Kneel in sorrow,
And then confess: we will still keep on—

Or as a hawk faced angel put it,
As it lifted me in huge brown arms
Above the purple hell of
Screams and murder in my
Dream left far below:
"Water, earth and sky
Are green and blue from here."

His wings were massive,
Red as sun struck clouds
Across the west above a storm—–

18

Big Morning

Big morning,
Too muggy for poetry when
The mad old prairie thunder
Storm rolls in from the southeast
And the black cat runs
For cover—
The sky is yellow—
The wind comes up—
Thunder crunch—
Right now rain would
Make the perfect beat
And write its own
Sweet poem—
First line?
Duck and run
Little folks below—

Here we come,
Across the hills, the prairies
Where we even make
The oil boom look small—
Pause, repeat, and hesitate,
The first big flash of lightning,
And here comes the rain—

19

Called in for a face lift, sinus strip or two,
Hair transplant, weight loss, religious conversation, too—
It was a 1-800 number, and they took my name,
Basic info, then the old on hold—
They got back on and asked me what
I was trying to pull—said no such person ever lived.
When will I learn to leave my sin alone before it all gets
    worse?

There is a chance that this can be—
We can imagine it on the screen—
One of us gets up late and finds the other
Dead as a rug on the bathroom floor—
The blue jays, out on the balcony in the
Sunshine, shout for their peanuts, now!
One tries a bit of CPR on the other one and
Can't remember how, and the flesh is cold—
Shock, first tears, fingers on the phone,
Three famous digits of doom and death—
Then with shaking hands, we place a
Towel under a head, or cover the aging
Naked beauty we have touched so much—
We regret again; we should have touched it more—
Pick up the toothbrush, lay it down
On the marble ledge and begin the
Stone carved dance in which we learn how judgment,

Mercy, Grace make death: and life of death—

20

Slanted Ads

Saw a thing on this page, said, open an IRA in minutes,
    thought it said, join the IRA in minutes, facebooked a
    note of protest about such ugliness, and the SEC was
    at my door for tea in 15 minutes flat—
USA—USA—USA, they chant outside the White House
When we take Bin Laden down on our way off the fiscal
    cliff—
I have lost all politics—I am compassion, shame, and I
Stare at the prairie to find my joy—an old friend said to
    me,
"Hey, if you can't sing it, you shouldn't say it."—
Now all I can add is, sing it and pray it—Peace, bread,
    peace,
Water, peace, air, peace, animal peace, plant peace, and
Bury your corpse deep in the ground with a digital screen
Slash The Air—today is enough if you cut the salt, fat and
    grease.
Feed the electronics to the gerbils and take yer air in
    through the nose—
Tomorrow is hard to spell and a gleam in some
    ambivalent creature's eye,
So let its promised parties, jams, feasts, famine, prophetic
    fandangos
Fester and fume away—promises are threats that failed—
The Past, fergit it kid—a dried up pea in the bottom of
    the sink—
Clean it up, wash the silverware, and warily smile your
    way
Into the next main frame—by midnight you might know
    the score—
Poetry isn't a book; it's a faithful garden walk—
And we shroud the garden, blood, revenge and blood—
Wear green and blue; believe in the heart that made the
    hearts—

Let the buyers and sellers suck their comic cosmic eggs—
Let the scholars explain—there's so little else that they
    can do—
Walk out in the snow and take the cold—I hear tell the
    "boom"
Is moving straight this way—get ready to write the
    songs—
Start with a wide old open chord and slash it big and
    wide—

21

The Kind

He was the kind that wanted to save the suffering
Beings of his world, but spent his best years
Only to discover that he was the suffering world,
Caused a good deal of the suffering,
Made himself the bleeding wound
While he found healing ways to make a whole world
    bleed—

He lived his life backwards in a digi magazine
Of fiber optic tinted photos, places, dates and names
And played the absolution game for gain, again—

When the snake gave Eve the apple
She obtained a monthly cycle and a watch—
When God closed down the garden
The clicks of sin began to tick,
And we became the kind that learned to hope, regret
And dream of failure all at once—

22

So what do you get when you add up three dead
    raccoons,
10,000 vanished prairie flowers,
10,000 roaring trucks along the roads,
Wind generators tantalizing you with blue out in the sun,
Canola fields to bright they look Lorca's lemon groves
And so much grinding traffic you don't know what to do?
Highway 2, oil land news, pumped out dreams and Eden
    blues!

23

Doubt the Woman In The Dream

That little darting butterfly is really called a moth—
On the kitchen window screen, it helps me to wake up—
The sparrows on the wet driveway
Work their beaks in passion, all their small aggression,
Total, deep attention to the insects as they strike—
The moth on the screen is perfect, still—
A mourning dove completes the sound against
The songs that float and fade down the distant hall

"Tear down those old grey walls," the singer moans
The morning dove sings "who, a hoo, a hoo…"
God, in covenantal mode, pulls out a rainbow,
Shaded, five deep pastel hues against a stern old sky—

It's all too much and tells too much, too much at once,
And the simple facts add up until I cannot show you—

In a dream disturbed by songs on radio this morning

I heard a woman's voice: "You think of self, self all the
    time,
While I can only tell the truth."
I wake up; I did not know; I still don't know; but here it
    is—
I doubt the woman in the dream, and I trust this day—

24

Blessed Are Those, Again

Then I must be truly blest—
Wallow like a mucker in this shitty world—
Dead babies, lying drunks,
Crooked bankers, broken, used-up women,
Beleaguered face book freedom fighters,
Right wing dingbat murder-loving thieves,
And that poor dead fox, glued down, highway flat,
Beneath the wheels of 10,000 midnight trucks—

25

Another fox that runs full out in fox tail grass,
The yellow, gold and red dust body
Runs and sways in a wind grooved wake—

So I think of your life now
The way the sunlight glazes and
And I can breathe so lightly on your
Sweet downed arms—
I swear we are still young,
And as I drift down these long dark caves
Below the Milky Way

I carry you along with me,
Blue moons, red planets and the stars—
Blessing, flesh, the fox, your wisdom tales
Until the moment when we cling
To Jesus' scarred and dusty feet—

26

Wallace Stevens Live

Some kind of theory journal small press
Funk about a poet standing by
A rusted orange wheelbarrow
After a heavy rain, and he knows
He has more dirt to move (not metaphors)
On a hot June afternoon,
And as he does he thinks about
The things so many readers end
Up thinking of and hopes they think
And know of him, the one who
Wrote the poem, left out the chicken
When the barrow wasn't red at all

A pheasant rooster saws a log of sound
In the weeds and grass across the road

The poem and poet, thus the reader
Will be gone
When the sound the rooster made
Gets caught
And runs on a spear of light
And the currents past the raft
With the boy and the man named Jim,
And then we're out into the comet's tail,

And we get Sam and Wallace Stevens Live—

27

I Am Not, But

Start with currents from another poem,
Wet grass, damp air,
And the two fawns leap and tear
Froth the air around the doe
Across the road out in the half grown field—

Fireworks, 6th of July,
High Summer's stupid, noisy declarations—
A waning moon pulls up out
Of twilight and lifts up its face
Into the star-slashed deepest reach of sky—
Orange, red orange,
And then the Kill Deer and Night Hawk songs—
I am not Aaron Copland—
I am not old Van Gogh—
The song and picture stick with me,
In my head, my own thin slice of gravity,
Mass, and what I call gratuity—
But grace is never gratuitous—
It is always free and clear—

28

Then The Silence—Grace

And I have seen her move,
A surge of waves on

The sharply broken black
Stones above the sand;
Under the 50 mph
Canadian gusts that
Bend the bleak grass
Flat and bury the buttes
In six foot hardened,
Driven, scooped-out snow.

She can bend and then
Rise up and lift me
With tectonic shifts, the Creator Soul,
Thighs to pelvis, then to back,
Limber, bone on muscle, stone;
Polished, turquoise-eyed;
Concentrate into the
Thunder, shaken, bent;
The cottonwood that does not break;
Then silence, grace,
As the spent storm
Drips its last sweet drops from the sweeping leaves—

29

Lips cross the ivory, slightly olive, slightly
Curved out muscle near the navel
And drop down into the
Near mahogany,
Thick brush deep below,
Then onto lips,
The gates God's own temple court,
All the time be thinking hard just
What might she feel?
A desire to feel what

She might think,
To think she thinks,
When all the time you know, perhaps,
That what she thinks,
Is not a thought at all, but something
Lives right next to Wisdom's soul—

Oh the gates of the city
Where Wisdom waits:
"Let this fool in
To eat and drink for free"

30

Naming The Punk Who Sings That Song—

Bernie, Metigoshe one Sunday, 1979
walks up to me and my guitar
and says, You know, you really
play some kind of Gospel Punk,
which is what all the big guys called
me for back home for years,
Me the skinny, scrawny bird-necked
no talk boy, so shy, the one who almost
died and was too weak to carry a real gun: Punk

And then the first rock band to play
A grain elevator gig that year on the
underrated old west side of town,
the Remains, with epic smash up shots,
Satisfaction, Gloria, and the great old Midnight Hour
40 years beneath the mast,
far underground, outside the grid—
I surfaced, re-born, untimely ripe,

Billy, my papa at the old AMP said
in a post on a poster wall:
"Watson: The Oldest Punk in the Magic City"

31

Humans and Sacrifice

The doe? The one you saw
With her two leaping twins
In the green field picture
Before you knew the last shot,
The final frame that came?
That doe was hit by someone
In a pickup pulling a boat
Headed north from the lake
Just after dark last Saturday night,
And no one stopped, but
Someone nearby heard the thud,
And the doe was found,
Pulled off to the side of the road,
And two fawns may make it yet,
But it's only a matter of time
Before the body of the woman
Will be discovered down in a ditch
By a half sun-cooked road worker,
Tired on his mower,
Numb from the hot wind that
Sucks at him every time another
Semi howls by and casts a black
Shadow over the road shoulder: now

Moonlight Becomes Me

I wake up sweating from a dream
In which my tongue is
Filled with quill-like steel needles,
10,000 stainless stinger needles,
So I choke and gag
And cannot speak,
Must pull each one out
With my finger nails, one by one,
And each barb tears my tongue
With pain so electric I weep

Awake, I go upstairs to the wide open
Window room, and it's washed
In the light of a near full moon—
I sit and watch, and feel my tongue,
And know the taste of steel, still there
I lean back in the chair
Stare hard at the cloud-hung moon,
Trust her intentions once again—
"Go to sleep, no pain," the moon will sing,
Bing Crosby's moon glow voice—
See now, "moonlight becomes me"

The Sound of Early August Rains

Yesterday and then again today,
We get the green rains of June
In the first few days of August,

Just on the edge of the next great drought—
A draught of silver grey pours, then
Hard showers sluice off dust:
Yellow lawns, tree leaves curled up for autumn,
And house roofs, streets and cars—
Will it do any good out in fields
And pastures already yellow and dry?
10,000 sweet wet hammers beat the roof,
Drum on the shingles, windows and walls—
The amazing water runs down the gutters
And into the streets—
It's not too late for the doze, the vision,
The dream, the sleep, and half-awake time:
The sense that water speaks to water,
And our bodies contain small lakes and streams—
The dry land itself is the bed and shores
Of an ancient secret lake,
And the source of the silverfish green
From the huge prairie sky is…
The largest, lightest ocean we can ever swim—

34

The Shadow of the Lord

"…and be sure to greet your neighbor and have a
meaningful conversation."
—Preacher at the end of a worship service

God's conversation is not meaningful—
Meaningful is all this "feely feel",
Temporary, tentative and tame,
A passing comfort to the brain—
Get to the point of love, She says—

Get to the meat, the dirt,
The shocking smack of truth: proclaim!
There is no point, no proof, She says—
The picture is the point,
The play, delight, or death!
The mystery at the heart of this:
Inside the frame, up on the wall,
Within the canvas, in the paint,
A texture, sweep to tint and tone
Where the ache of recognition
Meets the ache of loss and joy,
The momentary sense:
We say, "I see; I hear." Believe—
Soul won't seek instruction:
Assembly manuals in many tongues
Will not insure the Kingdom Come—
The keepers of the Mystery must not
Define: they defy philosophy in order
Just to help us see the shadow of the Lord—

35

Like Elvis

I wanna be like Elvis
Shoot my TV set
Do myself like Elvis
Am I a fat boy yet?

Politics of Elvis
And join the FBI
I don't like them Beatles
I'm gonna be a spy

I wanna be like Elvis
Make those ladies cry
Live down there in Grace Land
Although I don't know why

I want Elvis hips
And them side burns too
Die there on the toilet bowl
While I sing the blues

But I live in the Bakken
Can't even pay my rent
Out here in the oil fields
In a plastic tent

36

The Salamander Nature

The stolid salamander out there in the silver rain
Cannot cross the long grey place
From a water hole to a distant smell and not...

The grey squirrel chased down by the lean black cat
That has grown up from the kitty play
Cannot avoid the clear and panther truth...

The grey white man with the gimpy leg
And swollen foot or the spider that gave
Him the bites cannot decline to somehow face...

And see:
The salamander nature, the beast's own
    comprehension—

Wonder isn't quite the right response to all that is
    revealed

37

A Kind Of Face: Petra Dreams in Bonetown

Slow learned, late-bloomed,
Autumn baked enamel blue sky
Stare makes a kind of face

38

Love That Knows God's Ends

The genetically male guy who plants the seeds
cannot know the fire and pain when the seed explodes—

But like the frightened child,
he can be drawn to stare, even as he grits his teeth
in that grinding action between miracle and shame—

She spreads her legs like a bull rider,
but she herself is the furious love of the Cosmos
that expels the new thing into life,
even as the urge to nurture makes her muscles
clench and release holy milk—

And when the little one walks off up the street
alone someday,
only she will know the impossible burden
of love that knows God's ends.

39

The Mystery of How I Stay Alive

J. Buffett—B. Dylan

As useless as an empty wine bottle in the street
on a sunny September Sunday morning—
don't ask anyone to live with your
daily disasters
And raucous, wrenching resurrections—
Only so many times, the rolling stone,
before folks want stability—
Then the yellow leaves,
in the perfect, still morning
release like dry birds launched
from the cottonwood branch—
The air is yellow—
The grass is yellow—
deep in the clay and
rock on the shores of this
ancient river bed,
the roots are drunk and dream new green—
Here is the mystery of how I stay alive—

40

P'sing

A Psalm for the non-believers
They live so literally
Always tip toe on the surface

They will not drown in the depths of God

So they will not know their garlic souls
Socrates was light—
Blind on blind they lead the
Closed eye right into the hole dug for a grave

The miracle in the dark chocolate hole,
The burning cold, center of the Cosmic core,
Is only theirs by grief and grace
They go there shocked in disbelief

41

Psalm For The True Believer

Nyet! No, Russki Farmer!
the childish finger that proves how God exists—
Nuts as the childish rebellion that says there is no God—
We know nothing just when we know too much—
Wisdom is to help the fool—the smart ass burns
In his own hot air and hell—
Box Elder bugs are smarter—
Crows and Blue Jays are all insane and holy
From staring into the face of the living Lord—
It is not enough to discover the bones
And myth behind the mystery of the tale—
Science re-discovers what any eye can see—
Humility explores the world the eye can
Never see until the eye lids are pulled
Shut by some hand that touches
Vision and the dead eye sees, out of breath—
The duped and deluded pay the bills
While the Sexy Goddess Blue Jay Beauty

Arrives shouting at dawn after sleeping
The night in the womb of God—
The truth of God is not a thing
Observation or denial will ever possess—
We will never know this God,
This God that clearly knows us all—
We are not here to possess
But to be possessed by this–

42

Resurrection comes in Blues

She's an artist of change—
She walks her way across
my Sunday morning grey
with her flute in one hand
and her soul in the other—

I have seen her lips—
I have seen her fingers—
they always move me—
nothing is ever improvised—
Even when she pretends
Her grace is the judgment
of Wisdom and the
wings of Blue Jay grace—

My stomach, head, and
power to charm are gone—
I could watch her play for
hours, but she is as humble
as the willow across the street,
bent, down low, tensile steel,

and since we are on the line

I need her worse than death,
and still must admit that
I have to know her ways—
Love is less than four letters
and big as the Sunday blues
So she says to him—
"What, you got yer self all saved?"
He says, "Yeh, I am, am on the way."—
She says, "You read the Bible?"—
He says, "The Bible is the Word OF GOD!"—
{Here I am—creeping on up on the children, here on old
    age—
help me pay attention—
Give me the curiosity to dig
through the warehouse of
leaves the trees leave on the ground—}
So she says to me—"Yer haircut is odd."
I say, "You a barber?"
She says, "No, I am an institute of taste."—
Samson moans, looks for the pun—
Her apples are so bright and young

43

Let me see the shades of
white and grey October
when the sun comes gold once more
let my hair down,
set my Bible free,
From empirical dust and literal rust,
and fill my eyes with light,
all leaves, and

high keen prairie wind
so I say, "I know: Nothing!"
Call me Sgt. Schultz

44

Our Singles Dance

This Saturday October light
before the human noise and blur,
becomes the time to know a thing or two—
The grey squirrel, Blue Jays, and then I
have found a way
in early sun above the bluffs
to share the peanuts,
watch each other, stay alive—
The squirrel, a thief,
sometimes a meal himself,
Is careful, fat, fast on his feet—
Bandito Blue Jays
come and go, scream hello,
get real bold, beaks full, down,
and soar away—
The squirrel makes
mad dash, jerk dance on
across the sunlit, shadowed boards—
What's the deal? He knows
Death is never far away—
Fear is just the ruined light—
So we do our singles dance together:
wary, lively, not alone-death's door

45

To heaven's quirky gate—
Canadian Cherry-oak
and poplar leaves hang on,
let go, and fly from green to red to gold
Until the boards are clean

46

Always Those Last Words

When the cankered Chancellor of that false education
    called
death comes pounding on my chest, my dignity, my work,
I want one day with you, whether we speak or not—
my fingertips, my tongue and lips will leap like little
monarch butterflies, like the sound of the Blue Jay's claws
When he lands on the deck to eat the offerings you left—
So when the dark comes down and spreads from the west
    like
A slow moving ocean of blue, red and black,
I kiss off the educated guesses, hired guns, millionaires
cannibals and bloodless gasping digi-ristocrats,
climb up in the old dark bed of resurrection eve
and write my stone in God's own words:
"in the beginning was the song",
and you will write below: "there you go, you always
had to have the last word, the last word, here again",
and I, "there are no last words, lover, only the words
that come before the light when we will be the Words"
I hope you weep right when you say, "last words, last
    words,
always those last words… "

***

I Hate To Insult The Dog

Despite the fact that we haven't had a doorbell in over 4
    years,
Dude still barks at the doorbell ringing on TV.
—Veronica Pinnick

Despite the fact that my gun-toting AR 15 loving cousin
Has not had sex with his organic just turned whole food
Hippie poet wife in 4 years, every time she looks kindly
On him, he goes for his automatic weapons—there is a
Connection here—but I hate to insult the dog

It starts with four pheasant roosters across the dirt
Road at near dark
They crack and crow and strut around
As if they know the light
Hits their bronze and red feather dress
Perfectly right to make them cocks of walks—
Then later the two separate packs of unseen coyotes,
One in the east, one in the west,
Yowl and yip and harmonize,
Sounds like even the old folks and
Babies are singing out tonight
Next the first northern lights of
Summer, green, yellow, blue—
Isn't that enough? Of course—
No camera, Facebook, foe or phone

Poems For The Man With Gold In His Veins

1

Look at the old woman who hated the syncopation
play that mandolin so loudly it turns into a
nuclear harp with 10,000
strings and shatter her ear bones until they hear!

2

Forget the momentary lapse of healing
There are two things:
The whimpering of the coward
And the weeping of the
Grief-strung soul
Little to both matter,
you will learn to laugh as well as weep in tune
shatter her ear bones until they hear!

3

Think, The Kingdom is here right now—
healing is here in the midst of the dead of this world—
The dirt itself holds the microbes that kill
And the miracles that heal

4

I miss the fresh cow piles, steam rising
Out across the yellow pastures at sunrise,
The end of October,
And the cows, ambling along the path—
The organic center of God in the middle of nowhere—
The man with gold in his veins knows it true

5

The man with the golden blood in his veins
knows the folly of youth and age,
the fractal break between life and death
the meaningless negative of positive voodoo,
the positive charge of the fool on the hill
that only music can understand,
the loop in the lines of time and death—
So when he sees the ornamental apple
tree stripped bare of yellow leaves,
missing the useful blossoms from spring,
he sings and praises the dark shinning
branches and dark trunked holy mahogany
ebony wood with its own melodic joy,
and he says to the world in his song,
We are all being healed until the day
we die, and then we will all be
brought back to life in body, blood
with fingers that dance on mandolin strings—

6

Drive down the highway to find a flickering screen

and a story that makes you hold each other's hands—
go golf with cards to get some META air
some philo-furious wind in invisible leaves—
celebrate a day of no needles but those on the pines—
eat a meal with no interrogation of veins
while the inquisitor of illness lurks above your heads,
but most of all, give each other a kiss and a poem
and escape through the hole it makes, the kiss
and the metaphor until you get to the
weekend place where the loons call out,
the water is all October clear,
and you can lift you faces up to the dizzy moon
and howl like the wolves up north!

7

Be Well, Be Healed, Be Well

On Saturday honkers form up, fly south
overhead, over heard in the soft-hazed blue,
and music is live, in blue a bit too—
thirteen wild turkeys strut in the street,

the smell of stove smoke,
the ache in the throat,
the scent of wood and damp and leaves
when thick air floats, 64 degrees,
until the leaves are piled,

soot and dust, stripped lights and dusk
under October and the hooked, half moon—
the freights hoot, squeal, then pull through,
and the star in the east in summer sky
is the star in the west in seeping light,
and the man with the golden blood in him

walks with the girl with the golden soul
and the universe speaks in the
silent tongue—forever, forever again,
we chant, be well, be healed, be well, Amen.

8

Monday's Comin'

Church is ok—all them hymns and prayin' don't hurt—
But them eggs and cheese,
yellow, white and yellow,
hot like the sun itself on a nice autumn day
when ya got the gold in yer blood,
ya gotta eat gold too, mixes of gold—
ask the woman—she's mixed those colors for years
been through more paint
than you can shake a pallet knife at—
Ya take that Sabbath; you pray,
sing, rest and then, in God's name—EAT!!!!!!
Monday's comin'—beat 'em to the punch!

9

Out of Your Body and Soul

Behind the hot mask lies the chemo brain,
and it is ready to see some loopy things—
the odd bark of the crow this morning,
and what is the bird, invisible, always,
that quacks like someone is rapidly
bounced up and down in some old whoopee cushion
    joke?

Here it is, almost Halloween,
and there you are, surrounded by white,
sweating behind that mask—
Just shout, "Boo!"—Scare the hell
out of all the blue people in that room
and frighten dark molecules
out of your body and soul.

10

The docs and nurses can dance around the bed,
Speak in tongues of science and angels,
And you can ignore the TV,
But the needles, the bright glare of metal and plastic,
The alien presence, the jab, the pain,
The point where your nerves and muscles
Say there is something new in your body,
Well that just will not go away—

Memorize the shape of the mandolin,
The loop and roll of the rope-like melodic vein,
Where time stands still
And you know you are the one who is moving on—

Then slip in the ear buds
Turn Van Morrison up
Just a decibel too loud
And jig the melancholy, heartbeat,
Celtic, sea-rolling gospel blues
While Sister Wisdom dances along—
Healing is sweet beyond these songs—

11

Is that our Mother's Voice?
BOOM and shooting in through the cath,
like a mutant chemo-brained junkie's dream,
wake up and radiate one more day—
"Harvest and planting"
as if you were back on the plow
down on the South Dakota line,
but now it's the temple of healing
in a Minnesota valley that slowly
empties its October paint cans
into the river and brings on
the thunder and lightning storm
and the cold wind,
so the lightning flashes against
the black mirror windows
of the Temple complex sky line,
and dark windows reflect
the light that still will grow
even on mornings after winter slips in
on the clipper ship of white cloud and wind
from the Canadian ocean
and across the Dakota sea—
Show us all a song to sing—
a pizza and a bottle of red
can heal like Jesus' hand—
Is that our Mother's voice we hear?
"...and the Word became flesh
and pitched a tent in our midst,
full of grace and truth."

12

That Lazy Humming Golden Stream

They take the stem cells,
then shoot them back in—
the body becomes its
magical healing power—
It's a picnic with many
cancer cells—(ants, call them ants)!
until the power of the magic
eats the ants on the food,
a reversal, catches the ants off guard,
the way they tried to catch
your body in death, unawares,
and so the justice of nature,
nurtured by your own stem cell souls,
re-asserts itself and then heals,
makes you wonder,
ponder these things in
your heart, like Mary—
what powers lay waiting
to bring in the angels,
the kingdom, the great
picnic banquet down by
that lazy, humming, golden stream?
Healing completes us—
It's more than a circle;
this life seems to be a loop
that spirals us on to meet
ourselves the way we were made to be—

13

One reason I am here—

Oh, the cock crow of resurrection
With the cracking call of
Of blinding orange
Blood drop dawn
And the light on water and grass
Mercy is the heart of the prairies

14

We look for signs of life
while we dig post holes
in sandy, rocky, clay mix,
and the geese fly overhead
in enough arrow heads to
provide Christmas Dinner
for the entire
history of the world—
as snow begins to fall,
the white of spirit, death,
fresh air, hospital fatigues,
and then the sun comes
sweet and orange to gold
as it burns its way to
the west, the eternal Isle,
the day before Reformation
day, four days before Halloween,
and grace rest in life
on the edge of the witch's
broom, the coming full moon

and the light in our flesh—

15

Maintain, clean, keep it simple, uncluttered—
Say if it's your birthday and a full moon too,
you'll be fit enough after howling all night
and chewing the moon in your old hairy suit,
wake up with rabbit fur (you hope that it is)
stuck between your blood stained teeth!

A 95 year old woman told me
she's got a new summer hat for next year:
"So, do you think I'll live that long?"
She says, "Arlene, you know her, Arlene?
Well she's 100 and bought
14 new hats last summer,
14 new hats, and she says she'll
wear them all at least once."

Halloween comes two days past full moon
I sashay all black and orange in the light,
the warmer than usual trickster toned night,
and in the morning, wretched and white,
I'll pray to St. Bridget in golden sunlight—

I live forever, in step with my hat
in a mandolin heaven and loop
my way into something that
keeps the gold flowing like
fire and sun in these eternally graceful hands—

16

Forget about the snow—melt, slush, dry and gone—
the fog is so thick today that the lights
in the valley are gone from view,
like in the head, the chemical stew,
and then the steroid driven jumps,
the exhaustion that makes for dread—

In the temples of healing kindness holds the tone—
watch the thick fog, inside and outside the head—
be a scientist and the experiment all in one—
then the fog begins to lift and everything
turns a pale gold, then deeper in, the
gold that pours from the grail of light,
and deeper still, the holy water that turns
to golden blood in your hard-wired veins—

Forget the Halloween teamsters,
the All Saints Day saints kneeling white—
It is gold that carried the king
(Frankly Stein and Myrna)—grace, just grace—

Cunning as a Blue Jay, gentle as the
turquoise on the breast of the dove,
goofy as me, me a dirt dog on one too many bananas,
Sing: every dog monkey gets his
Bananas it his own banana tree,
slow as a turtle who knows how to love!!

White to Gold to Blue Jay blue

17

Wash The Darkness Down

When all else fails, eat to
placate the spirits of light—
feed them what they love—
stuff them full of bright food—
the apple is a sigh, a dream,
a bad choice made,
whatever drags us away from
the food we need to live—
feed the spirits six times a day,
the hours of the times to pray,
the hours the sunshine
lover spirits come to eat
and build up their guts
and muscles into shape—
then they can slap the
demon, dreamin' dark heart
dead wood spirits down,
dump them in the river
of the blood and let
them drown—flood the
river with prayers of gold
and wash the darkness down—

18

Now dark morning All Saints Day,
orange lights on the balcony like little teeth,
and plastic bone shaped lights
glow within and radiate against the
Jack o lantern's golden skin—

Jack says, no, I am not bad luck: all right?

Eat and sleep, eat and sleep—
the chemo halo around the head
like a crown of glowing thorns
woven from old barbed wire
loops and tangles, dreams and dreams
and the prayer, $E=MC^2$, space and time,
space and time and not a loop,
parabola, parabola; the fence
line dreams its tangled way
across the plains that look
like North Dakota, Argentina.
Parabola, Parabola;
Someday the lines will
meet in healing Kingdom Come—
goblins and saints all dance as one.

19

The Old Philosopher's Stone

You let the blood heal
and turn from light to dark red—
you sleep while it bubbles
and sings in your body,
pounds with the magic
of healing in your heart
and veins, a cleansing,
a fire bomb bounce of
those magical god tricks
the old magicians dreamed—
The temple of healing
gleams like a shining

black sapphire rock
in the middle of town—
Lean back, close down,
let the loops uncoil, and
you come back surprised
at the green light against
the whitest snow and lights—
The temple is in the
heart of your prayer—
turns out that God has
named you to replace
the old philosopher's stone—

20

God watches over, whether we like it or not,
in ways we do not like or do, or not, depending—
Daredevils say the roads are fine—
Sane people stay off the roads and breathe free;
the dogs are quiet after the first snow—
the silence outside, the muffler job of
an inch or two can sweeten the sounds of a
Friday night in Boom Town, Bone Town, and
the sky is white where the light hits
the thick moisture dripper clouds—
Ice forms on the head and streets,
and you try to breathe in the fog;
that is not the heat in the room;
that is the heat in your brain and soul—
God does something whether we like
the weather or not, and not is not
in the nature of fire that rules
the galaxies long on their looping spin,
and the galaxies might like it or not,

but they have no more power than we—

Hiccup and Heaven

So the battle of cell to cell combat goes,
spurred by something as simple as a
hiccup that never, never stops—

There was a dream-like moment in
between the spasmodic rise and sag
of organs, nerves and tissue—
there is the bridge—
there is the river, and you
take the moment and see past
and present layered against
each second there, double exposed,
and you can walk in both at once—

The Main Street buildings,
new faces, new paint on old walls,
a few grassy, snow-covered
vacant lots, and the Spots
where faces you knew look
strangely familiar, your friends
and even your own lost son—

Suddenly, there you are on stage
in the old Play House theater,
and seated in the audience too,
and all the matters of life or
death in your small town memory
super impose upon each other,

and everyone in the theater
becomes everyone you have ever
known—then a hiccup, and sure
enough, out on the icy road
of your prairie striding heart
you decide, again, you and
your friends, and all you have
ever known or not,
all of a sudden you all
decide, then and there to live—
New Heaven, New Earth,
holy Jerusalem on the plains—

22

In and out of the color crashed fuzz of talking heads,
numbers, election night wizards and crafted hysteria,
the chemicals ooze in and out of nerve endings,
in the blood of the body politic, and the bacteria,
introduced into the heart space of the republic
by an unknown host and carrier—yes that bacteria,
too small to register, but for the slight fever right now—
this bacteria the size of the horrors of the Hades
on the slide beneath the microscope in the
hospital lab—bacteria, fuzz, fur like the tall
grass in the pasture, yellow and wet and clotted
with snow in the "seasonal mix", the bit of ice
that yanks the car towards the ditch and back—

Heal this land, the mind, the memory, the broken
promise marred by greed, fear, and dis-ease,
the things that seem to be changing too fast—
God does move in mysterious ways, so let's
not dare to make decisions for her at all—

23

Look Out The Window: Alive

We confuse the Kingdoms of God and earth
with what we struggle to do to survive
and call the process staying alive—
Inspiration and despair both come
from the unseen, golden germ of truth—
the battery dead, the car won't start,
the kids won't behave, the illness is chronic,
the congress is peopled by culled out steers
that try to give the Bosses their milk,
but the teats of mercy are dry, dry, dry—
we, wet-wrapped in the arms of disease,
the abstract large canvas of cause and effect,
hurricanes, defections, insurrections, great calamity
that tear up the power and shut down the grid—
officious, arrogant, colonial leaders are
imported by elected officials, appointed,
campaign cocked fools from the fool farms out east—

They say we can go home soon,
after we stamp out one last insurrection
imported from the powers of the air—

Our skin is glass smooth—
we are haggard with hope,
numb with desire and healing—
we stretch the loop that tethers
our brains to this world
until the loop ought to break—

we look in the mirror for a healthy one
and see our souls are
translucent and stronger than death—

Know this: the judgments and
mercies, the I AM we named God,
are the mystery of grace,
and we write many books
to explain them away,
but the face of grace
is the fact revealed in one song—
Look out the window: alive.

24

Mighty Nordic Skull: True Love

My head shines on in the light of God
in spite of the two-fisted storm ahead—
I cheat at puns, and defy straight lines,
talk in loops and equations while
the people all nod and agree with my
words, when we all know the secret
that only She really knows is hidden,
for Her alone, beneath shinning skin
and my mighty Nordic skull: truth love!

25

Stay Put, Be Still, Be Flesh

Prayers circle around like
eagles looking for a snack,

the light snow, piled high
under the yard lights in the street,
like a loop de loop, again,
that ever recurring dream of
a plot that has no start or end
where time sits still,
behaves like the myth it is,
and the complex sins
of our desire to heal
end up looking silly as they are—
the wind is getting stronger—
Stay put, sit still, be flesh—
the Spirit will blow you home—

26

We Are Always Going Home

Then comes the bridge between the battles
and the thing we call going home,
when we go with the knowledge of
sure wars to come, the road that
goes from the life line on the palm
of the hand to the etched lines,
like cables on the map of the prairies,
and those prairies have gone
from 100 shades of yellow and gold
to the pure white, the black-etched
bare trees, the blinding sun
and ten billion stars at night—
and home, and going, and healing
and rolling along with the gold
in our veins is somehow new
and some way never ending,

even as friends, lovers and children
help us carry what we thought
we needed, and never needed at all,
help us carry what we have learned
and will take with us to the stars—
we are always going home
apart in a moment and finally,
together, always, for sure—

27

The Beasts We Dare Call Friend

Night comes down—
the dark glasses come off—
the vampire of the state line road
takes on two quarts of his own blood,
but leaves still pale from the gold that
burns in his veins and wracks his cells—
he drools his way to the nearest real
burger place and takes one red and rare—
with a smile like a snarl he tells the waitress,
"you can just skip the bun!"
Consciousness, survival, and joy are all the
hints of the great day yet to come—
until it comes we live in ourselves and
the hints of love that lurk in nature's beasts:
the beasts we dare call friend—
The sun came out today
and sprayed gold cells of light across the cleanest
new born snow of a completely empty and healed
    mind—
the toxins floated, frozen in the air above the whitest
Disney Snow White North Dakota drifts ever made,

and you looked at it with the dark eyes of a new
born baby hearing the words "snow" and "white"
for the first time: pointed out by the tip of your
mother's pointed, wiggly finger—
Time, rivers, blood—
your home is swept clean of dust and cobwebs,
clean of all but the howling laughter and the
wild weeping that you have kept there so long—
it rides the dust motes across the clean rooms
in the sunshine and soaks into the walls—
Come home with your blood vessels of gold,
your mind of silver and white, your heart full
of fear and hope that comes close to revelation—

28

God Made Real

So deep in the prayer that the bad dreams seem new—
long past the point of wondering what you did wrong,
you find the difference between justice and mercy
then the road to home is cleared by light wind and
    breeze—
the apparatus, the rooms, the personnel and clothes
will live on inside your gleaming brain—in this valley,
the coulee—no—over to the left, close to the crest
of the skull where a tuft will grow when you learn
that all along you have been a bird with hidden wings—
just think, all that planned stuff, and the point comes
clear where you know that ten million things happened
to make it possible for you to be you on this road now—
God is not a "be"—God is a word of "act", from
before there was until the you who is right now—
You are, again, I say, the dream that God made real—

The Holy Old Child Once More

You got four times the power you need little wild man,
Four times the little stem cells to make you new and nude
with the fire that started you down the state line
across the pastures and through the buttes of the
true west river all those loops and lassos ago—

Home is across the grass lands and over that butte
down into the valley of the Mouse that roars—
Bone Town is ready for your new flesh and blood—
This morning three huge raven arced and curled
the air above my round house—"Yah, hah," they
    laughed!
Good luck ravens in the bad luck goofy world—

The woman who nurtures, cries and smiles
in tune to the mad music your face muscles make
when you look wise and refuse to talk?
There she is, ready to roll on along that line—

Old Cohen the freak Rabbi has got the sisters
of mercy kneeling above his wounds and fears—
Here come the daughters of mercy for you,
and they will ride you home underneath the
thankful skies and into the Advent snow:
You are the holy old child once more!

Go safe, go slow, go far
the Italian airman said

as Hemingway toed the trigger
and Pound went off to jail
and Henry James pondered
Venice without pants in the
window of the old hotel
But the man with the
gold in his veins,
he got off the killer roads,
into the temple of healing,
across the concrete fields
and only gave blood to live
Thus he shall strum his
Mandolin when others
are dancing in their graves
and the wheat will wave
to the west river mandolin wind

30

The man with gold in his veins
is used to the fact that he glows in the dark,
that fear is light turned inside out,
that words are lies that become the truth
if they teach us how to live, love, eat,
drink wine and sleep with a lover,
that he has the power to dream his
songs in his sleep and know that
the mandolin, in its case
900 miles away from him,
will play along—and since he is
radioactive and cannot fly commercial,
he grows wings and flies to the
polar/truth north of God
in these dreams where the mirrors

only show what the Word has made,
and his mandolin strums and hums
like a woman in her sleep,
holy woman, wisdom, next to him,
awake, wide awake in sleep

100 Years Of Briefly Noted Eternities

Black Friday (ala Steely Dan)

When Black Friday comes
Won't bear no stocks and news
Go watch the people
Buy and sell the blues
When Black Friday comes
Pirates share the fruits
All Christmas long they
Sit and count the loot

When Black Friday comes
I will be the news
And before the lord
We all will speak the truth

No one gets to buy me
Go ahead and try me
Thankfully, I'm valueless and me
When Black Friday comes
I'm gonna climb a tree
And fly away and dream
My Shaman dreams are real enough and free

***

Self-consciousness

(False Consciousness, says Tom McGrath!)

Is as useless to creation, the hungry nations and dogs
as a piss in the Blizzard of 1963—
Go take an anxiety pill—
Awake, bless this world anytime someone breaks free
      enough
to see the whole ball of spinning Joy in the hands of
      god—
Adam gave names, and Eve gave birth, but who will
give up the face in the mirror and look out the window
      today?

George and Joanne out on their skis in the woods,
the barking dog chasing the trucks in the snow,
the apple tree across the street, cloaked in perfect white
to contrast with the perfection of leafless deep black
      bark?
The box elder bug on the floor by the wall
Sits and looks—does it sit and look at you?

Now that we've made it past 12/12/12
and well on our way to 12/21,
now that the Mayans have run out of stone,
and we are already in free fall
under the parachute wings of Grace,
far over the edge of the mythical fiscal/judgmental cliff,

See? You and the bugs are made of the same sweet
      stuff—
we all get the Son of Man or no one—
So bless it all; it all looks back at you:
Community, the dance of the stars
the jig of the neutrons, the Angels Singing in space,
just beyond the visions of black holes, fire and ice—

Steal Time
For Kate Barnes

The North Dakota Humanities scholar
In the Starbucks near the Capitol
On Sunday morning late in June
Prestidigitates and pokes a keyboard
And makes words hop on the lap top screen,
His yellow pad and pen on the table,
A book opened up between his arms

He's re-enacted Jefferson, Roosevelt,
Some Lewis and a little Clark?
Sock Jaw a Wee Hah is all that's left?
He hardly seems to be in the room,
To know me at all (since '71)
When I call his name
Out of the "distended and stretched out" time
I roll and thunder in his mind—
Then he smiles, nods,
And dives back into his mystical letter dance—
Who will he bring back from the dead today?

***

Paid Political Announcement

I follow my coffee cup around
the house first thing, the morning—
it can get better, but if it goes bad
at least I've had a holy start,
so if the black cat from next door crosses my
path again in the street, I will kick him—
he is the one who needs to be afraid—

the early light across the valley is orange
as if the last of August leans
far enough down to drop its
Muslin, humid cloth over earth—
take the Bible down from the shelf—
someone is trying to speak—
this is not a paid political announcement—

***

There is No Death In The Tower of Song
(Leonard Cohen on the occasion of his not being dead)

I think he's still alive.
There is nothing reputable to suggest he's dead, at least,
Says my son at the end of his investigation and prayer—

We would believe that
If someone was not dead, it should be a hymn of praise—
So why was it called a eulogy?
His poems sing like songs from the Zen of Days,
Mystery day trips, Jewish sightings of God in flight—
His songs sound like blues that would have been
Written in the key of this Creator's Spirit breath—
All mercy is color; all flesh is art,
And even the darkness demands the light—
Lighter than Lorca, simpler than Dylan
That deep Solomon bear of a voice proclaims the
Forgiveness, judgment, redemption, that is;
The defeat of the human illusion of time—
Leonard eternal, be ever unchained, in image and light set
    free—
There is no death in the Tower of Song.

***

Briefly Noted
(For Vladimir Nabokov)

A Dutchman who lives in Vermont
Claims the wind generators in North Dakota
Have killed 28 Bald Eagles—
When to have prostate and colon checks,
Which cancers will kill you,
Before something else does the job,
And how far should they probe?
The war will not be over when we withdraw?

How we vote on Measure number 4
Will affect the voters in Minnesota:
Religious Freedom distorted into
Insurance coverage for birth control—
The constitution groans beneath the weight of delusion—

******

Voices After The Flood

First of all
Last year at this time
Birds of all kinds were flying into
The big windows and killing themselves
While the flood water swept
The valley away in brown and sewer gray.

Second, I had not noticed that the
Canadian Cherry at sunset—

Birds and all
Became an etching,
Black leaves and branches,
Black brushed in birds,
The kind of black lined etching
Where the artist lays the lines
Against a blue white wash,
And an aching green,
So you think of eternity, lost or gained,
And water is not the issue at all.

Third, the little black cat is one year older,
Claims our yard in his patrols,
Notices me watch him
And makes me laugh out loud when
We play hide and seek in the window—

In the meantime, people down in the
Flood zone are taking
Weed whackers and brush cutters
Into their flooded out, dried up
Washed away, drowned out
Overgrown yards—

***

First Day of summer: Birthday

I heard you speak to me in several tongues:
Fury, the voice of the whirlwind, your faith,
The song of fire in the burning bush,
Your sex, the Song of Solomon,
Your promise in Proverbs 8,
The whirlwind about Sister Wisdom's head

There at the city gates
While the oak in the fire burns with
With the heat of exploding mistletoe
That makes the cedars of the badlands
Skip and leap against the rainbow
Curve in the wind at the end of a storm:
And all from one born in the flood of '69

*****

Floatation Devices

1

My tears wear steel jackets and floatation devices
That bob and float beneath the melody of every song—
My brain is a single, empty space
Inside my words; when I turn to go
There is the still and peaceful place—
My once manly plumber is unstable in the flood tide,
And each time I see that I love you,
My plumbing drones on like a drowning
Bag pipe in the lock below the hill—
The strange tree, June green, across the street
Has morphed its leaves into a thousand
Glittering white-green stars in the late afternoon—

2

Defeat? That's easy—it leaves deep holes—
Nature has dealt us some torn earth—
The scars tear off and reveal running sores—
Victory is glorious—we think we know this

But you end your time in retro-prospect,
Maimed and torn all along the way—
We share this earth, a common grave,
A grave of dust and clay, then space—
I wish to become the kind old man
Who floated his ark through the flood,
Who knows his kind and kin and makes
The motions, good grace trained—even
The devil can drink a nice cup of tea

3

So she says she wants to fix fence on her birthday—
This may be a metaphor—with her I never know—
These dried out broken cedar planks and posts,
Screwed and measured, pounded in,
Will stand back up and do their jobs
She will give them one more year to work,
And when the June storms gust and hit
At 50 or 60 miles an hour, they
Will bend like a wet green willow
And stand at her pleasure, against the storm—

4

Testimony, Evidence and Dear Old Shaky Grace

Sympathy and mystifications all subside with water—
When God's own time reads off the flood,
and the land and water are filled with soggy books,
it's a simple song, one note chant:
She says, "Sometimes I look at this flooded
House and smile for the shock and nod my head."

Melvin says, "There's 14 houses, no electricians
and the mold has to be cleaned out first, anyway."
A woman nods at her ancient husband:
"He keeps on driving down in the flood zone,
But he can't even tell me why."

You know where those streets end up:
Knee deep in weeds, mud marked walls
Empty windows and broken down doors—

A 14 year old boy: "I've seen a lot in these
Few years of mine; Gordon died, and Grandma,
Uncle Harold, my school's flooded out,
The whole grove of trees are chopped down,
More stupid motels and all these trucks,
Oh yeah, and then, the flood; the flood"

The Flood of Bees will come with spring

As the fireworks implode on my eye balls
In the dark living room outside the great windows
All across the valley in percussive surround sound,
I see the day is bracketed,
Plotted, a Ray Carver story meets the Beatles,
"I read the news today oh boy…"
The 4th of July was allowed to float by
In quiet tide of dry air and sun.
Then I watched the local news—

Physicists, ignoring the Bible and Bin Laden,
Discovered the glue of mass and weight,
The particle someone named "God"
Which means the whole meaning of energy changes
(God will remain a mystery though),

And the wild haired lab coat with a German accent
Says, "a woman in the supermarket will see no change at
    all"
Then there's Byron Pitts of CBS news,
In Western North Dakota—
A boosterish boor, political man,
Tells Byron "We need this oil boom or
Our small towns will die",
And the pretty mom, two kids, small town,
Says, "I know it's selfish, but I think of the
Kids and just wish the whole thing
Would go away,"
When suddenly, there he is,
The professional Humanist, re-enactor,
Writer, producer and
Thomas Jefferson Talk Show Ghost:
Byron: You, (the state) are envied by all—
Scholar: The coffers are full,
Unemployment is nil, and it all depends
Upon how we handle this thing
(Cut away to the natural gas burn off
The broken and crowded schools,
The people chased out of their own homes
By supply and demand and jacked up prices,
The small towns running short on water,
The highways, pavement beaten to dust,
The trucks, the pipe lines, the drugs,
The guns, the 30% rise in crime),
Ah yah sure and on and on in line.

2

So we go for a bike ride
Up past the airport, past the

Free 4th of July air show
Where thousands have gathered
To see the planes fly for free,
Up out of the valley that
Drowned out in the flood
Exactly one year ago today—
We ride to the by-pass
Out west on the bike path
Where the town grows north
And away from the floods,
Where the red wing black birds
Trill in the low sun,
Where the sloughs and hay
Fields turn into
Malls, markets and condos,
Then back through the valley,
On quiet streets
Shadowed by oaks and elms
Where half the yards
Are filled with debris
And weed patches
On flooded out lawns—

The jets of the nation
Fly overhead
In amazing formations,
Making maneuvers
That depend on that
Particle, barely discovered,
While below we pedal
Our way back home—
Now I sit still,
And midnight comes—
The full moon is up—
The fireworks die off—

The freight trains glide
Through in the valley below,
That low strange sad whistle
Where the tracks near the river
Were under six feet of water last year.

Flood of Bees

You have to watch this wooden tub for a long hard time
    on
Humid wet days, or dry like this year before you can
See a bee and study how long it takes to put on a nature
    load—
Oh they are deep, deft and dangerous, in and out
Of so many soft moss rose blossoms—
Last year when all the flowerbeds flooded out in the
    valley, the hungry bees evacuated up the sides of the
    hills with that deadly buzzing sound and onto the
    flowery bluffs—They tore at the flowers, instinctual
    pillagers, and there was no joy in the honey brown
    river under the mid-summer sun—

Deadly brown water, and furious flooded out bees at work—

The hammer, the chainsaw, the hand and the carpenter's
    hell. The bottles and old newspapers, history stuck in
    flooded out walls, Red and white balloons and the
    Halliburton Senator leading the false cheers as they
    tore the guts from the valley town—
If I sent you a blue, express letter notice,
It couldn't be any more blue
Than the blues I played on my black guitar—

Out in the weeds, among the furious bees
Wild flowers of mutant breeds grew in your drowned
    back yard

Paper Punch Effect

Good fiction is like good love:
It is merely honest about the poetry of fact—
It's that old-time paper punch effect—
3 sets of holes through 100 cheap sheets of paper,
300 little circles, spilled out, perfect in
A random messy pattern
When you drop the machine on the floor,
Each a perfection of sorrow
In the cycle of roaring destruction—
I see a seemingly random river is done—
If we are angry, we need to be—
If we grieve, we can claim our grief—
Time to get at it:
We will mount up and head west again in our hearts,
With wide explorer grins in our teeth,
No more of those grim evangelical faces—

A circle of sorrow to count the circles,
To circle the sorrows until all sorrows
Circle back home in this chant—

Who is the fool who said we all dry out the same way?
We don't heal the same, or grieve the same,
Or need to be saved when the water is the law—
Link the circles to chart the chains of design on the
    floor—
Then break the chains and listen to the sound of the
    ancient bees—

St. John dressed the Word in a seamless garment of
    grace—
The Word needed rain to fall—
Philo dreamed of how the Word uses flesh to make
The flight, the flow of what Luther calls, Spiritus Creator
(Christ fills creation like a basket is filled with bread)—
You cannot strip away the flood, the flesh, to reveal
The secret of Spirit—the secret is bedded in the flesh—
The bee is buried in the blossom—
The code on the paper is buried in the tree—

Jesus spit on the dirt, made mud, yes mud and
Opened the eyes that were blind from birth—
The Brooder bird took some clay in its wings
And shaped its Spirit into the limbs of an image of
    God—
Even after the rainbow is set in the sky
You will not understand the flood at all—

100 Years Of Briefly Noted Eternities: Bone Town
   Turtle sends out Praises
(Ken Rogers)

On Second Thought

All We Are and All We Have
do not remain the same
So who will I be
When the place changes?

I looked up Grandpa Mountain
Down in the North Carolinas—
Then I looked up North Dakota,

the N's, You know, two N's
Down in the SW corner
Where the dirt road heads
From Mott to Lemmon,
and there's that little jog
There was what I had
and now "I had" is gone
Instead here's all I am (I are).

Third time I've seen the Oil come
Third time I've seen old Bone Town down—
here we try to raise
the valleys as the Bakken
lowers hills—
When the Big Shots all repent:
wonder where the wheat all went,
where the cows all grazed,
the oil blew and pumped out black,
kids all moved to someplace else—
Supply demand, supply, demand,
taken by the unseen hands,
and I remember what
Eliot, Missouri boy once said:
"And Know the place for the first time."

So "some people have a calling",
sometimes tripping, often falling;
how deep do we need to hammer
in the cottonwood sun dance pole?
or a willow into the ground
to make the earth stand still?
The only straight lines come to us from the cottonwood
and willow post—
In this place we call a church.
God's praises penetrate the earth,

and all the rock is medicine,
all the rock is bread and wine—
Big oil comes to homestead us
until the one time harvest ends (Mike Jacobs said that of
    the coal)
they cannot know of the churches,
cottonwoods, and willows,
stones, or bread and wine—

The depth of this place is space and time—

So I offer once again,
economic development,
broadside on, sword or pen
supply and lie, demand to win:
Oil and steel make wars to win the world
while workers beg and bow before the
Blue flat screen of dead imaginations—
One more Missouri poet, old Mark Twain:
"Let us abolish policemen who carry clubs and revolvers,
and put in a squad of poets armed to the teeth
with poems on spring and Love."

This Is The Present
That was not snow we saw this morning—
The rain was so happy it splashed the
World with the transubstantiation of matter
In a glittering gauze to protect the
Naked, barely greened up earth—
This is the present, a gift to April 16th

Holy Wisdom does not do business cards—
She walks around in rags, eats food raw,
Pushes a shopping cart, makes all men nervous,
Plays in the fields of the Lord, listens to old Jazz,

81

Dylan, The Beatles (a lot), acres of Bach,
Reads Phil Dick, goes to odd plays in strange places
And never ever gives it up, the play—
When she's not in the garden with her love,
She rides the lighting into the Dakota earth,
Delivers babies in mud huts,
Swoops on the whooping cloak of blizzard winds
Out of the North West and into our hollow bones.
She plays our bones like handmade flutes.
She's so deep undercover, even she is not sure where she
    is—
But she gets the job, it's done, forever,
Before the foundations of the world, without end,
    AMEN—
Woman, you are perfect for the part—

***

Shades of Shadow Blue Maroon

The old blue turtle
In the blue-green grass
Near the brown/black
River in the blue white night
Of the pale blue moon
Sings a Grace Note blues
Tune in ¾ time to the
Turquoise silver of the
The late freight train
At 3 am as the rails vibrate
To the aqua steel
Of the clack, squeal, roll
In the brakes and wheels
Outside blue Newell

North of old Bear Butte
His shadowy pines
Will point us down
The long blue funnel
Of the Milky Way to the
Swirl and strings of the
Ancient waltz in
Mary's robes and swinging
Shades of shadow blue maroon.

Come Bear Witness

The screaming Blue Jay on the railing
Does not beg, demands instead,
And when he gets his peanuts,
Breaks them, gleans them in
With gleaming eyes,
Four or five gluttonous whacks at once—
He glares at you,
And that is all he does—
Thanksgiving never fills his eyes—

Even Orange moss roses ignore your gaze
And the great yellow blossoms
On the un-named weeds along the street:
The vaster vegetable indifference of nature—

And the doe in the late evening light
On the neighbor's lawn
With her twin spotted beautiful
Princesses playing at her flanks?
Watch her ears prick up—
She knows and sees exactly where
We are and examines our desires—

When she knows we are lost In praise—
She continues to watch
But ignores our wonder
With her perfect assumption,
The insights of a magical queen,
And slowly strolls down the empty street,
Her well-behaved royal
Children process along behind,
Through the unmowed coulee
And into the wild trees—

2

And a mud brown rolling river
In full flood, boiling out her
High gumbo banks,
Sweeps garages, decks,
Garbage, houses, years of
Graduated incremental humanness away—

Stand on the dike as it washes away
Dynamite, beg her, curse her, pray hard and weep—
The river didn't know we were there—
Mercy is not a thing she was made to give—

3

The Dragon Flies do their work overhead,
Impossible intricate flights on blurred wings—
They might as well be a flight of angels
For all they care for the flood down below—

It seems all nature knows—

We humans are here to witness
And that alone—
She has no time for our worship—
You want to worship, she says,
Go find yourself a God—

*****

One Year after the Flood

Here it comes again—
be blessed in sorrow my friend,
the doorway, street light
at twilight—
Walk out in the evening
Beneath old rose skies
The color of water
Behind your drowned eyes,
blessed and alive in the end,
Ready to swim on again
Grief will not be denied.

Cold Lonely Mountain
The older one gets,
the more one practices the subtle laughter just west of
    bitterness,
just east of empathy, ahem,
as one sees another mind wrapped in the clotted clothing
    of
vita/resume/rigid-amour-gouts-license-e-,
pass the tea, dig out the Cold Lonely Mountain books,
read the lovely calligraphy of the new year sky
as the stick branches clack out a tune for god—

Tree of Knowledge: Good and Evil

Old Adam scorched me
Eve made a flute of my bone
Then the ate my apples
Snake says all evil is gold
The guardian Sentry
Stands at the gate
While I sag full of apples
And die from the weight
The story is old
The curse is all true
This ancient red magic
Will happen to you

***

Grammar of Grace, Again

Mr. Watson must pompously correct our grammar—
Ahem—When Jesus has the right view of you,
You can't help but worship—
There is none more worthy, the singer sings,
And what you gonna do when
The Hound of the Kingdom
Holds your body in his teeth and looks at
You with those big brown hunter's eyes?

***

Redemption Is At Hand

We have come to that time when the last

86

Box elder bug is sagely and safely in the house—
Ice, rain, sleet and snow challenge our denial of nature—
The box elder bugs wander around, harmless, irritating,
Black and orange pin punch notice of advent,
Anxiety, apocylypso strains; summer and autumn
Wear off, anybody still raking leaves after the
First ice and snow should be examined by a
Jury of obsessive/compulsive recovery groups,
And the wonder of the darkest day,
The longest night might just surprise us again—
That blue star is a planet—the fox and the cat can
Share the meal of fish on the shore, and children,
In spite of Black Friday, in the presence of daily
Good Fridays, continue to expect the Coming of the
        Lord—
When that happens, lift up your head, fear not,
Your deliverance is forever drawing near—

Black, red and grey, when blended with
suffering, wept tears and howling laughter
turns a holy green,
and then the Holy Green
shows up at your door
wrapped in a toga and combat boots,
says, "Hey, what's for breakfast?"
Behold—look up—your
redemption is at hand—

Even When We Curse Her Names

This morning the Angel in charge of the night wind
That connects earth to the cosmic realms refused to go to
        bed—
She gusted and blew, wild and roiled under a strangely

Elfish hooked moon shook Christmas lights loose from
      houses,
And polished the streets and the snow—
Then the Angel in charge of paint for the morning
      decided to steal some giant kid's pastel chalk—streaks
      of soft green and purple up against each other,
caught and held in a usually impossible orange—
Childish sentiment, sediments of shades—
But now, the pastel Angel went to bed,
And the blowtorch-er air-brusher Angels are out
With their fires and gusts of power,
To blind our doubts with fire and faith,
That verb for despairing, crooked, blind, dumb and bold,
For all wrong headed inquisitive fools—
Ouch, I can't see; I can see! No I can't; I can see!
We shout to God even when we curse Her names!

Talons Wide

…. you been gettin' around again—luck, curse,
      serendipity
All too often called God's Will—you, me, the stray dogs
      at the road blocks, and the survivors of shootouts,
Plague and the never quite ended holocaust—

My Grandma always, always said,
"There but for the Grace of God go I,"
And My Mother too agreed—
"Grace covers it all because none of us
Knows why things happen the way they do."—

The cracked pot, the prophet, leather-skinned
Old wizard with the broken hand, cracked,
The chipped, tan ceramic mug you use only

When you are sick; you drink a certain kind of bitter,

Honey sweetened tea that your ancestors supped from
    that same cup—
Here come the certain fragments, and broken
Phrases that tell us the world is smashed and
Put back together, but never right, always judged
And dying, and yet, there! Still, it floats, beyond
The reach of the righteous Judge, maddened
Murderous rebel, the hand on the torture switch,
That patriot with his automatic weapon set on full bore
    kill,
That circle of sweet, dead children, all our babies,
Laid out on the school room and shopping mall floor—

All the same—the stutter of violence and shame,
The bellow of the jury and the jaundice of the judge,
All in the glare of the all-seeing eye—
Yet still she comes flying, naked face and chest,
Inner thighs and arms, all incarnate flesh,
But she wears an armor of angel feathers,
Helmeted, back like an eagle,
Wings like the ancient birds of myth, she comes for us
    all—
Grace and Grace, ice, air, water, wings above occluded
    earth—

When she swoops down, talons wide,
There will howling and tears of joy—

The Prayers of Lorna Kelly

And she looked across the water
and she saw the story changing

89

when the lepers went to holy light
and died in heaven's arms

She made charity her family
she let wisdom guide her mercy
and now she stands before you
with her arms all filled with light

Oh The Fire that burns the Spirit,
Even in the winter Sun,
She flies and leaps in a way that
Makes an eclipse hot—

Into amazing angel dance!
She opens out the book,
Takes off the torn old veil,
And then we learn to dance—

Last night I dreamed a female Bald Eagle
Devoured an amazing bright colored
Long tailed bird in an old Chinese Elm tree—
I ran to get a shotgun to try to shoot the eagle,
But an old man kept me
Until the eagle flew away
don't tell me nature's purty—
Might be beautiful, it's savage
In its glory, savage, bloody and unsparing—
Is that what you call beauty? Yes it is—

***

This Second Would Be Enough Forever

Angel back with pastels again
Light just right,

Charcoal lines of light posts, wires
Between eyes and sunrise—
Two crows, side view; still
Silent, they search the valley below
Until I look to see what they see,
The three Godheads of poetry in your life
(Oofta, yasure, and bygum), spoke and agreed—
Half the time poets get so caught in the window dressing
They forget when they kept it simple
And let the light in the glass—ooh—I made that up—
How is this—all poets are detectives,
Tons of details and clues,
And the unsolvable mystery of existence—
Ouch—made that up too—too much Borges,
Too many years around the Soul kill machines,
Not enough seconds here in heaven.
And this second would be enough—forever

***

The Crack Pot Wizard Song

This gig really sounds fun-and ding dang diddle,
Too far away and I'm a crack pot wizard solitaire
With no beard that I can grow
I do not know, I do not know
I'm High on stress and low on magic,
Got nowhere to go, nowhere to go,
I did sleep studies in magnolias
A long, long time ago, time ago,
But up here in the winter hills,
I just know, I just know
If I wave my wand I'll have somewhere to go,
But there's always one more spell
I need to know, need to know

Before I know it's time to go,
Time to go get on the train and turn her loose,
Turn her loose, turn her loose
I be the grey man in the green hat,
Ridin' that caboose, that caboose,
I'll be the grey man in the green hat that rides on that
    caboose!

The moon is up in the middle of the afternoon,
much too soon, way too soon,
hear my Daddy yell, we got a job to do,
and that means you son, that means you,
too many black crow turkey buzzard songs,
been cold way too long, cold way too long—

***

Redux

Tomorrow looms—
of course the man with
gold in his veins reads
another vampire novel—
gold and blood just mix
in old souls and veins,
and the snow is a back—
drop for the red and gold
as they bleed out new
air and life into the black
pumping heart of oil country—

A cougar northwest of us all
lifts his nose to the wind
and sends the scent of
oil, blood and gold in

mottled molecules across
the white lights in the sky—
Plato is an exercise of mind alone
and cannot heal the body
or this broken, dinosaur land—
Of course the music is the thing!
It makes those molecules dance—
Nude life is the end we find begins—

***

St. Patrick 2013

fer Jimmy Joyce and his drink of choice

whin yew ere a servent it is easy too doo Joyce's cheaply
like yellow peepking cheeks and tongs under the hem, er
way hear the hemerignway, at them Theme Himingstien,
say Jimmy Joyce to Ernie in the bar of choice in grey
paree along eh scene the sane, the siene siening fer fish to
chip intoo the poeme he called the Wake about the first
of the sleeps of many long and feminous slip and sleeop
of Finnegin never to come, to come again, again again,
unless ye believe, you skinners, has beinners and sinners,
in the incorruption of the lard Cheesus fleshly fleshy
res—erect—now it is all too easy to pun, but not so
easssssssssy to come! To the conclusion of the pair au
graph Jimmy Joyce followed like the mighty mousey liffey
kind of runny guanines fer a guinnnes muddy brown old
Source of the souse to to the sourest of course—and it
ain't Play do, play to—if is clay we rise, reselected—black
jesuits be damned/the pope eats Jews and beans and ham
hocks up to the hocks of the horses legs in the muck and
mud of the brown and tan to bring us the legendary
Emerald EYE-L green!!!!! Let the Green Man Play!!! St

Patrick, you hater, mad hatter, destroyer of Snicks in the garden of breeding, bleeding the blood of CHEEZUS down to yer feet, some feat, that, and back we go to the beginning in which is our end of TS Elyot's, tough shit Eliot's finale line along the cups and silver spoons for tea, and tee, on the course across the gulf o yrs.' tilt me see that this Magi magical manicaal muystery tour continues from the docs of and Caverns fog Liverpool to the meat and potatoes and wheat and snow of the vent at the center of the new world—rugbies is the game—now the minstrels should not have names—and the man with the Gold in his veins, the servant, not a lover of the serpent—rattles snakes on the butt of the butte above the black devil town!!! The servant, I say, to go one his way with his fingers stroking the sting of the strings on his 8 stringed harp and hart, the fleet and flying melodic mandolin!!! Stys pater nester addict's day falls like a grenadier on his grenade at the battle everlmore and always in between the Word and Byrd ye see?

***

Here's the good thing: Redux

the man with gold in his veins
looks in the mirror at the
complete ageless mystery novel
of his own face,
wonders what is going on inside
his bones and veins,
picks up his mandolin,
tunes, strums and the
spirit comes
here's the good thing
she makes his picture whole.

God is the Dead Man Walking

Even a death sentence on the block isn't for certain—
Our own diagnosis is often close to what we call fate,
sometimes a fat buddy, sometimes a skinny geek
in a B-movie cloak with an ancient harvest tool,
sometimes just the blink of an eye and gone,
sometimes the length of War and Peace in a Day—
We are all half-finished, half raw design—
We are all precious all of the time,
and time is never lost, instead it wraps itself
around the spiral of chromosomes, yeast,
fungus, giant trees, continents, climate change,
the inland sea, and the moment you find yourself
in the mess of what you did or didn't create, and
the second you do or can't get out of at all,
History is never done, never repeated—
It sweats for the future—
Indeed the Kingdom comes,
but we forget it comes to us all—
Death is the moment we forget,
and then it is God who remembers—
God is the dead man walking,
The giant cross above his head,
The legions of life above his strong shoulder,
Even after the Temple has been destroyed—

2

Don't know what causes the inaction on my part,
God or the Devil hard at work
in the guise of someone's foolish fear and hope,

and you do have to wake up singing,
especially if you think you been sinning,
the only bad habit that will keep you alive—
just lay around the shanty,
lean back in the in the old broken chair,
and then have the faith in Grace to shout,
"It's time for someone to come get me out of here."
This will work in the spring when even the
robins are shocked and stung by April sleet and snow—

3

It is coming, like Summer,
Like High Summer in the Hills of the Elven Queen—
like a dumpster dive in fresh vegetables,
like a sunrise in a flower garden that mosquitoes cannot
    find,
like a Jimi Hendrix solo at sunset,
a single guitar note sustaining over the heritage park,
like Main Street on a Sunday morning with no trash,
Like a Ray Charles record at midnight on Third Street
in 1946 with just a hint of breeze——Pangea

***

Phenomenology of Heads

The black cat tries to jump up onto the backless stairs
From behind the steps, slips on ice, lands on his head,
Stands, glares around to see if we have seen him, fool,
Walks around to the front of the steps and slowly
    mounts—
The snow covered power line above the street
Drops a clump of white that turns into the wings

Of a soaring gull, then back into snow
As if to say, "Did you see that, what I just did?"
I know a woman who got what she flaunted
Until her man got all the mystery he wanted
And then rolled over to go to sleep—
What are you doing? He said when she woke him up—
Rubbing your Genie bottle, she said and made her wish—

The wild turkey tracks cross the snow-covered drive way
In the morning light, up onto the steps, and then they are
     gone—
Where oh where do stories come, and where do pictures
     go?
My brain is a mirror ball under the bright moonlight
Every piece of shattered glass reflects the mind of God—
Stare into my eyes—listen to my song—confession
Leads to absolution without one single greeting card—
Dance beneath my mirror ball, and do not doubt the
     light—See, you say, the glass if half empty, or the
     glass is half full—
I say, what is in the damned glass?, Who is in charge?
And who is drinking the cool-aid!!!!

2

God bless Charles Darwin—
It all began with a Beagle, a bird and a beak,
And now we heal our arteries with faux mollusk gel—

Sanctification in Incarnation

Nature heals even in the way she seems to kill—
Creation adapts to Grace

Somewhere in the skull—

Just dawned on me, why this hits so hard—
As a Lutheran I see Climate change,
Noah's Ark and Baptism all the same—
Triple vision of double-edged sword of
Universal law and universal Grace—
That woman, swimming, in the blue room filled with
    water?
She is Grace herself

***

Snow Again Tonight

The snow fell all night—
we were forced to sit and learn
and eat and be eaten by silence,
a communion of warm blood
the sun barely came up—
here come the dogs
and bosses' plows—
Why does someone
always piss in the snow?
Hope it snows again tonight!
Here's to tradition—
Scots/Irish with a good amount of
Frisian and Prussian to spoil the mix—
My favorite colors are green and blue—
All Celtic flags have blue and green in them
Until the Irish Republican comes and no more blue,
The flag of which makes me think of Borges and
    Argentina

Every year at the time of St Patrick's day
I eat Celtic, listen to the Chieftains,
Green Man and all their nephews and nieces,
Think of Guinness and Scotch,
Read either the Dubliners or Portrait of the Artist,
Along with some Seamus Heaney,

And for the week I pull out a song list, known by heart,
Of Celtic laughter and lamentations,
The oldest from the Book of Kells, right up to
Van Morrison, U2, McCartney, Joyce and WB Yeats,
ND Irish Tom McGrath,
Along with a few little bastards of my own—
I play them for me and not one other person
Narcsi-celtic alone-lines and tears of blue and green—

2

I seek a place with low lights
And only those who want to hear the songs,
A kind of Eucharist of kindred souls,
Songs, then silence, jokes, then a few laughs
And blue and green tears as we far flung
"ND is everywhere lost Celts" sigh
And look out across the Mouse River Valley,
The muse and mother we have come to
Call nothing less than our own Lost Colony home

3

See I know this poet, a young one
who was supposed to write this grant
and get the Gov to help lead the

high school kids to a love of poems—
Instead he went to Florida to
build a house for someone who
does not have a home—Dylan!
"Ain't a house; it's a home"
and Neruda! ...the family can't
live in a poem with no food and water,
so we build the family a home..
now is the time Joe!
House to home, give them a poem!
But you know, before this snow,
The new snow and 7 inches to come,
When we all got hot for the
First hush of Spring,
And life wasn't Lent, a loan
Where we gave up green forever amen.

The south sloped down lawn
Was sprouted in something
Close to what you would call grass,
And the rusty, ragged old Pheasant
Cock came with a thrust and a glide,
With a claw toed sneak up step
And his generous colors gypsied up,
But now he's hiding back behind
The old mock Tudor, fluffed in the brush—

Prepare your ripped and rugged call,
A "take me down from that god—
Cursed cross" of a cough and
A giant crow of a shout old bird—
St Patrick is coming—
The snake is beneath our heels—
I'll pour you a bowl full of Guinness,
And we'll reel and strut until

Heaven and Bridget know we are here!

4

Eye on the spider hanging 20 feet above the heads of the
    faithful
in the sanctuary—he dangles on the strand in the breeze
    of a fan
and God help the Spider if he falls, worse off than "A
    Sinner In The Hands
Of An Angry God" here on this Palm Psalm Sunday
    Passion Play 2013—
If he falls among them Luterans below he'll face the
    power of
Law and Gospel, Judgment and grace at the hands of
    elder saints—
Jonathan Edwards was kind in comparison to this
    delimitation!!!!
Worse off than an ATEISTEIA on Saturday night in
    Gommoron!!!
Worse off than a Caddylack Saint on a Cross of Gold!

I, with my man Tom McGrath, am a champion dreamer,
A super dreamer, with the keys to my soul on a six-string
    guitar,
And family of dreamers worldwide over who keep
On and singing along—I am the body that dreams in
    daylight,
In snow in April when the robins flock in shock
And the sparrows peck away at the dirt in search of
    spring,
And I say to you, Go and Dream and come and Live in
    the Daylight

Dream of the Kingdom, a potluck barbeque in the back
    yard with
Buddha, Krishna, Lao Tzu, Scooby Doo, Shaggy, Bobby
    Z,
Jesus and anyone else who shows—
Moses and Mohammed have lifetime invites, but are sour
    grapes and never seem to appear—
William Blake plays Black Bird on a lute
In the Scots pine above our house—
Dark Horse George stops by to lead the congregation
Around the keg in a vespers service of Be Hear Now—

***

The Pale Green House

The pale green house had a dark green roof in a grove of
Chinese elm and Russian olive trees—an old man out
front rakes the dirt and grass and lays out the spot where
the road runs past, where the flower pots will go when
the winter bones are gone—out in the alley near a lilac
hedge an old woman stoops and pulls last summer's
weeds in the beds where the flowers come in May—in the
shadows, light and shade, the last snow stands and slowly
drips and soaks the sandy soil—
You and I are in the house, in a kitchen space, white-
walled, a century old, clean as a church, where the breads,
all kinds, all sizes, piles, are laid out now, and we try to
see where we possibly can store the bread or where we
can take the bread to feed someone who needs the bread
today—
In the room down the hall, in the window light, a young
boy sleeps, then wakes and says, "Heaven is in this
house," and we say, "What?" The old woman steps in

102

through the back door, says, in a voice that comes like a
song from her wrinkled lips, "Heaven is in this house"—

Heaven In This House

A clerk in the store in the dream tried to sell me a blue
        book,
An old one I knew you would love
There in the walnut, oak, and musty shelve
Among those decaying word on leaves she said,
This will betray the woman you love—
The woman on cello in the string quartet laid down
        harmonic lines to
Wake the sinners and saints,
Walked up to me at the reception and said
When you listen to me you betray your woman—
The lady in black on the second floor stair beneath
The stained glass unicorn window light said,
If you rent the ground floor you betray the woman
You bring her to live in this house

I say to these dreams—
I do not step back in my tracks anymore—
I do not look three steps ahead—
Words, melody, the temple of home
Are the heart of the woman I love
Fidelity is my own bone and soul

***

Chick Crit

Here was something about white chickens in the rain
        standing by my old red wagon that made me want to

shoot a BB gun at the wagon and scare the goofy
things into life—therein lies the sin of childish human
    pride
Hope of Deliverance from the Darkness that surrounds
    us—Sir Paul M

Ronnie has a baby in her belly
And wild strawberries in the yard
I have a poem of hope today!!!!
There are angels all around our heads
and they are not precious ornaments—
they are made of judgment, grace
and unquenchable fires—

Our angels are working overtime these days—
We give Eternity new meaning, yes?
There is only so much living dust to go around,
according to modern Physics—
According to Revelation,
there is always new dust and light to come
and a wine jug will be passed all around—
There's no reason,
That I can't comprehend, completion...
Geo Rodriguez "There's no Reason"

Heart Transplants

Someone gave the old Vice President
A used and broken beating heart,
Anonymous and pounding—
It pumped new blood in that guy
Who in his system bought the
Americans and made us his dream:
A terror house where we're afraid

To fly our own airplanes,
Where we bolster up weird
Warlords and their vicious body guards,
And the country is a flood
In all the oil we can steal—
Our young and barely filled out
Half-schooled girls and boys
Go marching to his beat—
Halliburton, Halliburton!
Hail the chief with blood on his oily feet!

***

21st Century Preludes, Prolegomena, Prayers of
    Explication
Blarney Barney strikes again, to throw these words at
    God.
Rick the Richard Rychardt Watson Watkins reeks from
    raking wreckage.
Henry the Havoc reaker, Godric, Rychardt, God's wreck,
Son of Prussian Rheine Keys, Rheinhold, Big head
bowed, big heart baby Henry/Huey pound away,
Ponders, pulpit pummeler, kitara picking, guitar tricksy all
by ear: Son of Wyatt, Sonne of Walt, old Water boy for
she, holy Ghost, happy hunting hound of Heaven, crack
pot Henry, holy hack: declares himself the slave of the
Queen of God's own spirals, the paradox curve, the
parabolic lover of Infinite Space!

***

after Miyuki Miyabe, The Sleeping Dragon

(And I am the fourth person who would

Like to think it possible to look at another
Without revealing a thing, myself—
Introvert, abused until he spews the stews
And yet show them everything I have ever felt,
To thought to be, or not!
In fact I want to still reveal it all and yet
Have no one know it but God and me!)

***

Sorry About That But I Just Lost Track of Time

A watch does not control your time—
A five bedroom house is still in the middle of the oil
    field—
You sleep better when you are at peace and leaning
    back—
Or gut full of sad sack sorrow, leaning back—
The Awesome is in your genetic code which knows the
Number harmony of the sun and moon—
When you count you put imaginary limits on the
    infinite—
When you comfort, caress, walk away, or weep,
Satan will have no time for you—
And Holy Wisdom takes a day off to dance—
And sing with the village idiot—
The Buddha on the road defeats time—
The Christ on the Cross devours time—
You, in a song, make time stand still for Kingdom
    Come—

***

Osama Bin Laden and the Names for Grace

"Osama is dead, at Obama's hand?"
Asks O'Bannion the son of Watt Henricksen the Miller
Who lives next door to Reinke the farmer
And who knows how many other closely related names.
"All the world is a stage says Will, Sam,"
Said O'Bannion, "And the same for you Obama,
Whether you are in Belfast or in Bag Daddy, DC,"
And Reinke the farmer hauls his grain to the miller
So Watt Henricksen the baker
And café owner can produce the bread
To feed the world that seems to wander
In through the cafe door—

When Jesus died the media was all just word of mouth,
The Emperor didn't care to comment or to know,
And it took 300 years to get the story written,
And in 2000 dirty ears the poem ain't all come through—
From what we have seen of O'Sammy's ruined face,
Jesus is still the only one with a clue
What to do when the whole big deal caves right in,
And though some thugs will say, "Thank god,"
Some other thugs will call the dead man
A holy saint and a martyr, nothing is revealed
(So says Bobby D the poet, "Whoever he was—
Man we got no culture," Paul, Simon, not Peter).
We do not even have enough
For a tale for old O'Bannion to spin out a decent
Ballad for all the losing sides this time—

Remember Martin Luther King, Jr.

—Jesse Watson

***

Well Like Old Lao Tzu Says
Voice Mail Mac Print
(found hi koo)
It here in.
Report hold.
Noon.

***

Punk'in

Momma was a space cadet
Daddy hasn't landed yet
They're tangled in their safety nets
Cold, so cold, they're old

Momma take a look at me,
No more drool, top 40 dreams,
Ring tones and a big flat screen,
And there will be some more, and more, yes more

Tele-vision teach surrender
I will strive to be a spender
(All Ameri-buy-out bender)
Tattoo me, a nice nose ring!
Let me blend my gender—

***

To an Angry Brother

I read in a book of vengeance,
Sharp, static, hard-edged stones.

Brother why do you chain
God like a hellhound to
Anger, all teeth and sharp glass?
Why ask god the way you do,
To shred and burn the heretics,
Now, when you have read the past?

Use your burning tongue in words
To show your enemy the clear
Bell tones of Easter morning light.
Trust your Blood Hound, Jesus,
To sniff them out and lead them,
Wrists taut his toothsome mouth,
To the banquet of his will,
So when you pray,
"Thy will be done," you don't
Betray the savior in the grove.

***

Species Identification

My woman says, just what are you? I say, take your choice
or a combination of all—Religious Fool, Over-rated
Village Idiot, or dog gonned hound dog high plains picker
bum—She says, hummm, all excuses, and you seem be
resulting of a mutation of three species—I say, good
enough sweet honey—now come over here, put that
calculator down and give me a big kiss

***

Prescriptive Come Up Ence

Hang five inter-biotic realization of mortality

Lack of logical rules for eternal health time—
Finite + anxiety + virus/germ +/- lassitude and rest =
Existential dislocation in the human universe
In the temple of death, hooded and dark
And healing—prognosticated and cool
Describe me the people
Paint me a face
Then tell me what just happened.

Wren Boys Run Amok

A red belly cushion against the wyrds of Christmas
Cauterize this comfort and joy me boy, just joy—
Someone saw a crucifix hidden in a star,
Another in some DNA—same day—
How far is it from Bethlehem to Ramah?
Oh, mama, you do know the way to Ramah?

Shoppers, sloppy sidewalks,
Dressed in holiday pounds,
Gold Frankenschtien and beer mirth!
Black Friday's effulgence from sewer grates—
Notice this fact: no one person saw a vision, a
Palestinian baby wrapped, in a manger
Near the bombed out church in Bethlehem town—

2

Silver bells, sidewalk's spell—
Shotgun shells; reindeer smell—
Bang a Gong on sweet FM oldies—
I go to the corner behind the lit tree
And listen to my ancient Beatles' CD—

110

Magic, come take me a way

3

A catalogue of fond regrets,
Old lessons learned and not applied,
Ancient, painful ruminations,
Attempt recovery; oh, redeem!
Possibly 60 poor used years,
Alphabeticalmanac regrets

Repent, complaint, weak observation
From out here on snowy roads
Somewhere between old Mott the Spot,
Damascus on the plains—
Still waiting for that sweet old blinding light—

4

Strip the deeds we novelize,
Screen play, poem and dramatize—
These here is tired old bits of lies,
Can't smell the good out from the sad,
Catastrophe now seems mundane,
No thoughts, just voices lighted frames,
Stories of me I can't believe,
No beginning, middle, end.

Drive down this road, the pheasants rise
And run along the snow choked ditch,
The splash of color, blinding white,
The St Stephen's grave yard on the hill
The old brick Apostolic church,

Roman Cat licks just desserts—

5

Spiel this time-bound hide of mine, dear Jekyll friend,
Time clock time, oh measured time,
Is my proof of sin, origin and sin,
Primeval myth to history revised on digital TV,
Bunk and nightmare, Jimmy Joyce, Henry Ford and a
Down in the ditch to prove the original sin!
Minutes to follow old Aristotle—
Skid off the ice and into the ditch—
The arc of a plot is a son of a bitch—
Exposition, conflict, climax,
Denude-moo! Says the cow
Across the snow blown wire fence!

You don't fool me time, eternal nows!
Vonnegut, Hebrew, Hopi, Nabokov, old dead Tom
     McGrath!
Everything happened ever already is and still is now
And will ever never be imagined, happen up the road,
Back then, always will be up ahead: AMEN

6

Some Advice To My Fellow Coyotes
*(Facebook post to the ND State Legislature, Wall Street and
The congress of the United Straights—2011)*

We need to be fresh snow this morning, see,
If we want to work for a wind fall wind blown
Change in the way we run the hill tops of the

Colony into the days ahead us, or
We are lost to the world on the whole
They want oil, wind, water, children, too—

Snow glitters in the pounding light,
Powdered platinum beneath
The frost blue jewels of air above our lives—
Sneak the children out of school to see—
That would be more holy work,
As someone said, some thinker said to me:
Light on the feet, quick in to bear a soul,
Cold and strong as steel when you run!

But hear before you up and howl,
Oratorical idiots in the halls
Will not stand by while we get bound
Caught in mercy; justice, Lord—
They won't sit still while we play clown—
Record, denounce and document,
And finally nail you, terminal,
Total, tenured third degree—

Polonius was once the coyote
Politic, knifed through the curtain seams,
And furry Ophelia, fuzzy in love,
Got drowned for all her beauty—
Hamlet who should have been the best
Ended up poisoned, bloody, destroyed,
In that wasted final scene—

No—yes—maybe
Coyote lopes away to imagine the
Ways to keen in sacred winds—
Eat road kill until you're full,
Raid the dumpsters of Beaver U.

Don't eat poison, yip and yap
The slap stick gospel right out loud,
The rifles and traps of the bandit banks
And Wall Street rakes,
Bamboozler bureaucratic bums—
Coyotes run: duck for the bush;
Through your fur down in the snow—
Grow angel feathers in the dry hard snow
The Shroud of Turin is real—I see the stairs…

Long List of Human Schemes

Well, on the Sunny Day, wind from the south,
The early traffic on Broadway bellows, "Go!"
You can hear the oil wars from here—
The breeze is warm and will be hot—
A strange bird rings in the dead, dry tree,
Sounds like digital alarm—
The garage door jumps with the
Like the kick drum beat—
Two fawns dance on the lawn across the street,
Skittish, edgy, big ears high—
Smart fawns bounce for the coulee brush to hide
From the latest in the long and growing list of regular
    human stains

***

Bones of Poems

We ride on like the minstrels of the High Line—
We find where the sacred bodies lie—
Out along the antelope horizon—
Where earth and sky will almost coincide—

Who made the sky so blue and wild?
Maybe it was Mother Mary, mine—
Who breathes the prairie grass dance tunes?
Sister Eve I say—
She is the Queen of early May
Where I come from they call her Queen of days:
I didn't, Dr. Bones—
I won't, Worm bones
You can't, gravestones
Not on the red blood stones—
I take my stand
On Jesus' risen bones
And I do it always every time and only for the bones of
    poems.

"Le Envoi"

There was an old woman from Havre
Who married a zombie cadaver
It could be no crueler
They loved in the cooler
While he munched away and had at her!

Divination

I am of the clan of "an thitheir frith Brighde"
"Rathadach (lucky)" and "Rosadach (unlucky)"

A fair brown woman takes her stand by me—
This is a place, it was sweet to us—
Now it is fouled by nomads who turn earth black—
So stand with me now,

And we will make a vision
Of grass and rain and water right as God's green
    dreams—

Blinding Blue After The Rain
Mandolins, poetry, eight strings
10,000 leaping words on 1000 songs
In the lost colony of fear and illness—
poetry brings refugees home—
the hungry, wild blue jay
sings as sweetly as the Bard
shines blinding blue after the rain—

Boomtown County and Lariats in Flight
(For Seamus Heaney and Larry Woiwode)

1

God moment? I heard you say
This morning, by accident, I had the best coffee of my
    life
"Just give this new batch a try"
"Organic yet smooth and cool as Paul Newman's eyes"
But the results are vastly overrated,
Lost on my scarred and deadened tongue—
Look at the good earth we seek to destroy and remake:
Needle meta-catologic-file of catastrophes—
Oil, chemical, consumptive, radioactive heat and time—
Informational, experimentational,
"What I want is what I need"
Civilization, humanization, humanistic self-infatuation—
Lust and passion, logic, math and greed
(How many nails does it take to make Lord Jesus bleed?)
How many nouns and verbs do we find in that rusty old
Grammar of the Apostle's creed?
Self-holy dogma Darwin Deist jot and tittle?
Grace is only a five letter word—
It is noun and verb all in herself, name and deed her self
And let me live until I know her actions are enough

2

Just enough snow to cover dirt and melt,

To make smooth white sheets on the roofs
Of the house, across the yards,
So the darkest extremes of bare trees and evergreens
Show their inhuman art in a way
No human eye or camera can ever do—
All this against a solid white sky—
But I got up too late
That sand truck has already been by
And left a trail back to the human world—

3

God, not the Devil (that winged attorney gone bad),
Perhaps just an air current (I will not insist),
But something tuned into my petition
Or maybe it was a bare accident
(But there are no bare accidents, the scientist said to me.)
Well, something heard me—
It began to snow again, harder now—
The sand the trucks scattered
Is already buried beneath new snow—

***

I finish the coffee, black,
Re-read a few pages of
Kafka on the Shore
While listening to Glenn Miller,
And the folks do Danny Boy—
There is a gust of wind
Through the open
Balcony door, and then
The same wind hits the
Cottonwoods across the road

And down the hill—
There is a rise of pressure
In my chest, an expansion—
It is clear to me that
I need to tell you this
And then say good afternoon—
Yes the Cosmos is expanding,
And when it contracts
There will be no end to
The galaxies—
Instead, God will step
Out from behind your face
And say, "The pipes are calling"
And it will begin again—
And now, good afternoon

***

Always Coming Home Inside the Song

Joe says the first words of a poem
says he's always coming home
in on the currents of the place
from far away
while Nel packs up her bag
flutes, pipes, and whistles
in one place
says she's always coming back
and the man in the fedora,
that lady with the big voice
that guy with the blues harp
on this sunny afternoon
and the big man with the ukulele
tell us all that it is Sunday
and our seeking is soon over

while the kids all head back home
and we know well
that the music in the stillness
and the sunshine
is calling us together
from the chaos all behind us
while the light breeze
in the sky says the time is now,
always now, and someday
the music will just start up
and we all will be
always coming home
inside those songs—

Part II: Blue Jesus

Blue Jesus: Rising
A Mercy, Mersey Beaten Christmas

A Deconstruction of Critical Hairyarchy, Assess Ability,
Notional Assumptions of Heil-archical Authority,
A rejection of the Closing of the Books of Prophecy,
And finally,
A Sin-fishing Deep Gaze at the "was" that "will be
        Then"—See reality =????
The Rule of the "One" in our schemes,
The Now, as in Eternity—
The Kingdom Is Among …

To Jonelle, Brendon, all those who celebrate Christmas
with us—To the Ham, turkey, prime Rib of Beef,
Lutefisk, Oysters in stew and meat kin—To Poppa John
Woiwode, Blue Kachina McGrath, Little No Horse
Erdrich—And all vivisected Vegetable beings brought in
for the feast—to the Raven and the Black Wolf —And all
Sweet Things baked in the universe of Honey, Sugar and
Grain—To Tough Shit Eliot, Whiskey Holy Auden, and
the Lady with the blue lights down the street—And all
Holly, Ivy, Mistletoe, Green things/Evergreens,
Poinsettias, Blooms around the Ivy—Of plastic, metal or
once rooted beings decked and frosted, green or white,
that ran with sap or poly vinyl ore the ores of earth—For
Paul "unconditional" Tillich and the Wise Liverpudlian

Celts: John, Paul, George, and for Ringo who plays the tabor and keeps the back beat green and blue—And Bobby Dylan who thought the mop tops sang, "I get high," when in fact they sang, "I can't hide": both which should work for you and me, accumulated blessings of 2000 years of "here it is and not quite yet" and eternal coming of the Flesh Made Word Made Flesh to all— Comfort and joy old age, disaster and death—the Coming Life: Again

"hopes and fears of all the years are met in thee…"

{Old John drives north on 83 at a 40 mph clip,
Old Camel John in a shagged up beard,
Bald on top, and bald in tires,
Headed for the magic city, Advent, malls,
Crowds in the counting house and fears—}

And so this is Christmas, and what have you done,
Another year over and a new one begun…
—John Lennon

But as a madman's epistles are no gospels,
So it skills not much when they are delivered, says the clown
Open't and read it, says Olivia   (Shakespeare, Twelfth Night)

When Camel John comes, limping on his tires, limping on his soles, a pun for holy fun, he talks to himself, deaf as a Veterans Administration phone, and hears—when he hears, he speaks, and he speaks what he's told to speak, and might not know, and so plays the clown with a frown and they say he's bats, but he doesn't abuse the Irish fire, and he doesn't choose one mean word on his own, and (Poets utter great truths of which even they do not know the meaning—Plato) You Know Who/Whom—She =He=It tells him to speak—When God uses a human tongue 'tis frightening, but only for grown-ups—

The Gospels of John, and Paul, and the Beatles were all right—that is why I prefer fiction and poetry and song and art to so-called "history"—(Poetry is more important than history—Aristotle)—science and history take

123

themselves seriously; they have to, but the fact is that theology, the Queen of the sciences, is the study of the space where the HOLY moves into the human in word and act and leaves few tracks—teleology and proclamation are poetry learned by heart (Gordon Lathrop!)

My greatest hope is the guitar will one day people the West with African blue—Luther-zens, the so-called rural, so-called small, presumed-dying county lines of the Great Plains—

Here the cross and sin and grace are as real as a beer joint on a hot summer night—as real as the almost invisible secret trails along the section line sky blue jet contrails of our souls...

(By the way, I have seen snakes, birds, puppies, cats, pigs, cattle, a goat, and several humans die, slowly, and watched my gentle aunts, great grandma, grandma, and my own sweet mother butcher chickens with great gusto—death is real, great and ugly, and how we die does matter—I have seen shelter belts ripped out, and piles of dead trees left to rot in the middle of the prairie so a farmer can turn his huge tractor around in a "no till" field—death is sin—

Our Ojibwa friends, like me, are great meat eaters; but they were great hunters, too—the Natives give thanks to animals for lives, cull the animals from disease, and keep the totems of the animals for good spirit—we are all cannibals—life lives on death—The deer killed with respect is still a dead deer—that is no excuse for the horror chambers of feed lots and butcher factories in Omaha or where-ever—we should all have to find, kill, and cook our own food, clean our own messes—things would change—

What will it take? —If something feels wrong, it is wrong for you—and the earth will roll over our bones long after the wrong is buried—something as simple as love, a compassion for all things, seems deeply impossible and impossibly simplistic to people who don't know the back beat from Memphis/Liverpool, who have never gutted a deer, watched a cow give birth.)

We shot a few Eons in the nonsense quest to realize an ancient angst, an aboriginal truth, that the ancient souls (Camel John's sole?) were at least as smart as us—simple as the seeming pop of an old sweet song when the song turns out to be a Wisdom Poem—

I heard someone say, about Christmas Eve, "…will try to be drunk enough by then—I think that works—it is a long way away—I am in my hallucinatory stage, reading my way through final damned drafts all December— trying to make up for the sins of winter, or suns of winter or—see? Teusdee at 1 pm, cocktails in the faculty lounge with Nan…" The man had a PhD in Humanities and a bent for Critical theory.

{Meanwhile, earlier, back in the narrative drive, Camel John Haraldzen sticks his fingers in his ears as he rolls along and says, out loud, to an empty crowd in a silent car: "I don't want to hear it if it makes sense—I can't change it if it does—simple, that simple, my soul—"}

***

Only The Wisdom of the Son

What could balance the pain and absolve the father
For the failure passed upon a son?

Only the wisdom of the son—He holds his own child in
    his grip
And grits his teeth on the bitter taste
Of the young blood memory of the many times his
Hormones and pride made his own father pay the
    fiddler—
Under a skimpy blue spruce hung heavy with oversized
    bulbs in 1958:
A catcher's mitt rubbed with bacon grease and wrapped
    around a ball,
A thunder bungling electrical rumbling shamrock green
    football game,
Science fiction novels about the life of pilgrims on the
    planet Mars—
The main character's name was Camel John Haraldsen:
    from somewhere called
North Dakota, somewhere on planet Earth—

Advent Sparrows

…Not the humble kind—
But bold pagan banditos,
Like flashy monastic choirs,
Zorro masked in camel skins—
The kind of Baptizer birds that
Eat locusts for religious reasons—
These good-sized sparrows
In seductive black masks,
Full-blown white breasts—
These are no black and white dominos
To be tumbled by bad boys with BB gun musketatades—
They are glorious good sports,
Winter tough birds proclaiming their
Lusty tweets in the five below zero air,

Tough enough to tumble a squirrel—
They sing their folk mass from bare
Wracked branches—"Oh," they call, "hear one, come all!
Ana dominos dominius dominion
Repent! The Hairy God is at hand!"
Only those dumped on, dragged down and drowned in
　　ice and
Snow can hear and understand, — right John?
This is the advent allegory,
All about the sparrows and a much prayed for return—
Sparrows stay the season—Kyrie:
Give us the courage of the black masked sparrow
To sing, "Death shall have no dominion"
In the empty Canadian Cherry tree—

{Old baldy John, with his fur hat on,
Pulls his fingers from the deeply deaf ears,
Resigned to drift in magic down the road—
He is the bird who heard it all as if he were
The trunk of the worm-blighted, wind-blasted tree
Covered in black-scabbed cocoons
Of web worm crud—
Sit still soul/rest your soles in song—
Sing sweet Benedictus songs,
Stolen swiftly, winter wind:
So? Spring come early to the stable, home.}

Imagine no possessions—I wonder if you can?
No need for greed or hunger, one family again
Imagine all the people sharing all the world? (Lennon
　　again)

{John hangs on to nothing: woman, house,
Job or thought—John lets go, must let go and
Just goes on until the Hairy God decides to DO—

Often John sighs, but being deaf, can't hear it}

Duet at the December Recital
I once heard:

1

The woman and the boy sit side by side,
Shoulders, arms, forearms and fingers
Poised, balanced over the white keys
And slightly on to the black—
The melody runs into a canter then
They gallop into a key-tapped stride—
Their arms and fingers touch melody to harmony—
Light winds gust on piano keys: The snow?

2

A chestnut mare and
An almost-palomino pony
Explode out of the blown
Waves of snow
Above the crest of the river bank drifts,
Out onto the scrim of ice-trimmed water,
Across the shallows
And up out among black rocks
On the far bank,
Then out on the bluffs above
The river,
Back out across the waves of blown snow
Until the two horses disappear:
Sudden,
The white curtain of snow drops down—

3

The duet is over—
The pianists slide back the bench,
Step out, rise and bow—
It is Christmas north of Ekalaka, Montana,
North of the magic city,
North of Bethlehem as well—
{Camel John Haraldsen wakes from a daze at the side of
    the road,
Music as clear in his Hairy God deafened ears as can be}

***

Winged At Once

That laugh
Chuckles in my hairy ear,
Makes me want to be 12 years old,
Be the boy that fell
Out of the Wisdom trees
And fell in love with laughter—
So that now, this, later:
The laughter is precise
A moment, past, then present.
And there you go again—
Your own deep sound,
Sexed woman's laugh in angel wings and all
At once: Future, and then, Hence?
{Sometimes-Camel John, who can't hear himself,
Finds himself shouting a prognostication,
Top of his lungs, before he even feels the air
Gust out of his false teeth: as seen below}
"Happy Santa Lucy day you plucky snow-bound raven!

Even Tough Shit Eliot, Tom to you, would have it be and
    so,
'Be you new?' with the crown of fire upon your head?"
The red bird is happy in the wind-stripped tree
Even when you don't see it—
"Be you now?"   When the red heart beats in the
Branches you call ribs and bones—
What will it be, the New Year or the Final?
I am speaking this to someone,
(Old Camel John Haraldsen is my name)
Speaking to one, alone, but who?

***

"The Reluctant Reverend's" Liturgical Christmas Pills

Zantac: turkey, ham, sweets-sugared-fat to flour baked
Red-white wine-bevy of heavy bread—the beaker of
    brandy
Prosaic Prozac: the anemic cousin who steals the farm,
    the frosty sister who
Hates the season and makes it into a Lutheran lent; then
    the smell of lutefisk and
Dried carcass after several days of feast;
Zyrtec: after years of fine snuff sniff, the fake candle
    scent and certain kinds of ever—
Green; and the manger scenes are laid out long enough to
    need some dusting; they
Circle, buzzards-like, a herd of ghostly goats snorting,
    coughing, and weeping on
The bluffs above (Tommy Eliot in Rhame, ND)
Drop an X MASS medication smart bomb!
Try a stable meditation—
Take a star struck mediation, an

Old school Scroogie education—

Do not throw the stable boy away: keep the ox, forgive the ass, in a while it all will—Pass, and boil the fool who says "Christmas all year long" in his own Tom and — Jerry's—A maudlin Mass on X MASS eve with a prancing priest and Virginia's (A Virgin: pathogenesis of POP; dear Tom MACWRATH did say it right) And a power point on a twelve-foot screen with bits from IT'S A WONDERFUL LIFE —And the latest fading country star's holiday special on ICE—

***

I Will Take the Chaos

A piece of paper from a nostalgic fantasy desk: New Educational Theologies! Means, indeed, we are all are safe; Military, Higher Ed, and broken Banks enmeshed in fluff—The child left behind is pushed ahead to fail—The 3rd grade teacher thus resigned and—Took the job of painting private homes—Dean that knows, Chair that cares—The students, some, will learn in spite—Of grades: assess ability—Numbers, spreadsheets—Glib, and gibing—frequent-flying academic gurus—Senators, congressmen, don't heed to the call—Of old school Bobby Dylan; Logic looping legislators—Blood-eyed stymied PhDs—Who have never weaned a calf—Or dug another posthole on—The hottest August day—They spent their days in school—In the chairs along the darkened walls—And lost weight at the Prom—I have one awe full pun—Ass-S-dementia(A curse, a spell)— Here's to the Uni-mind: Those who seek to serve and save—And make and take control—With acronyms for

miracles,—Who paint red lipstick on the Poor Pig's
Snout!

"If it means less paper work,
I will take the chaos"—Buzz Light Year

***

Blue Light

At 4 am when I least expected,
I looked out the window
And for the first time saw blue light—
On the street, the snow,
The black tree branches…
A concrete drive, the roof of a house,
An almost full moon—
Last blue light, blue in the
Face of the one tall streetlight
Down on the corner—

In spite of the noise of
Street-scraping beeping sirens,
Snowplows replant roads
And trucks spread sand to fertilize the ice:
This is no metaphor.
This is all BLUE LIGHT!
So when the dark slim
Figure, shadow woman,
An ageless angel, flies down
From the top of a tree
(Somehow I know this,
Almost 50 pages before you do, dear reader),
Runs past the window
And down the street

With a dog beside her
And down the hill,
Why would I be surprised?
She and her hound are blue—
Miraculous visions do not wait
To come when willed, believed;
Asleep, with luck, called grace…
We suddenly come awake—
Black sky, blue mooned light,
So the snow blooms lilac leaves at midnight.
There is more snow since 1919, '49, '97
(Say this in the ancient quavering voice).
Some kind of accidental haiku here,
Or a sign from Old Tom Long Shanks,
Dead since 1993,
A sign from my own Saint Thomas,
As his dreams come blue, true, aged:
My thought is that this need we have for Dignity—
Dignity, sings Bobby D.,
This need comes from beyond
The old humiliations, playground, mud-puddle,
Brutal beating, other tortures of the beast—
This desire for dignity
Comes from ancient hope:
First not to be some critter's meal
And later not to make a meal for an angry God—
St. Thomas, your Kachina dreams were given you
By faith more nature learned than
All the world's great rules—
This night, the frozen earth can witness:
Moon and snow, sky turned blue—

So what can I give him, poor as I am?
If I were a shepherd I would bring a lamb
If I were a wise man I would do my part

But what can I give him—give him all my heart

In the bleak mid-winter, frosty wind made moan
Earth stood hard as iron, water like a stone
—Christiana Rossetti

***

Black Wolf

Everyone remembers me of something else
And somehow shows me truth—the way I learn,
Old Water Boy Haraldsen says,
And you, at first, I thought to dance,
No not that nasty Salome,
Nutcracker Suite, more likely,
Full-grace, laden, unaware—
The Burning Bush King uses
You as metaphor, mambo girl—
And so, uncertain, you do dance,
Tentative—what animal totem
Would my Jew-Cree vision use?
Black fox with a litter—
If you find the right line break…
In my sputtering, stuttering cadence,
Made concrete—
And let it run on paper in
A parabolic curve of line,
A fly fish line cast
Into water, roiling water—
The main channel
Runs too fast to freeze
Because the current
Is too strong for all this ice to hold—
And if the black fox…

{No! I have you—black wolf!)
Jumps that river,
Even black wolf, unsure if you can,
And finds your young pups living,
How could you, sleek
Long-tailed dancer, know
Your winter wisdom?

I knew a woman who window
Peeked the parlor of her home,
The tree, the gifts and lights,
Could not accept they were hers—
Merry Christmas and look out, noel,
For the baited steel traps, she says,
The blundering thunder…
Of farting yuletide guns
And the loping bluff-up buggering barks
Of drooling stupid hounds:
Their horny, musk
Snot snouts—
Gabriel is on our side,
Whichever side is weak,
And now unwilling for the flight,
Mother Mary knows the
Pondering, the ponderous curve of
God's loved belly,
Stumbling shepherds, sleepy sheep
Starry-wise astrologers, astronomers, all three,
And innocent ox,
Loyal ass are sleeping—
But an ass is an ass,
No matter which god it carries—
Listen, black wolf—
The Pillar of fire in the snow tells
Me to tell you to listen—

The frozen but running water,
The handmade fly skips on the ice
An angel fly in red,
The lights are in the tree—
Listen to the subtle sounds
In your humble fur and skin—
You are the sin of freedom,
The light of the distant star—

The blue star lifts on the southern
Quarter of the sky
In the half moons of
Deep December—

Never Assume

Sparrows in the bush
By the wall of the
Video rental store
May be Doing and Thinking several things,
Slashed flashes of wings in branches,
Brown and grey in silver/black
Against white walls—
They are hungry? Cold and crazed?
Or in my guess, they dance a parabola,
Guitar and trumpet tango—
They mime the roll of the Milky Way,
Yes, dance for God
When they don't
Even know one's there—
What do you dare imagine?
What do I dare to know?
Camel John, Old Haraldsen,
Bellows in highway droning dreams:
I am not here to tell you what to do—
I am being, to do what I can—
I am not about, all simple, to agree
To your attempted explanations—
Do I look like some professorial axe?
I have no hyphens, straight in line;
These little sparrows chained to words—
I am not charmed by your red-penned
Offertory hymns burned black on paper skins—
I am here for the compromise,
And thus, I am, my will, to die for
What I hear in my deaf ears, the words I still believe.
Never Assume—
I may just have to kill you on
The altar of The Word—

So, with the red fly angel and blue angel too,
Again I would then, when you were laid out,
Grow wings on my camel skin
And slowly fly away.

Any of the latter events would be enough to set a man
driving to North Dakota, ending up in a stranger's
farmhouse east of Minot, pleading amnesia and letting
himself be sheltered for the day—turkey day—before
regaining his senses and heading home.

–Richard Ford, The Lay Of The Land

—Is Camel John, Smooth-tired, tired John—Headed into
the Magic City, Oh Dream Of Jerusalem—Is he high up
on Highway 2 or headed north on good old north 83?

***

Mildred Drove the Mail
On the star route south,
Lost 7 sons in
6 car wrecks and
3 Great, gory Wars—
She took those curves
On gravel, grief and grit
And wore the rubber
On 20 tires down to wire—
The odd shaped posts
And RR boxes
Bent as if Picasso
On Jim Beam and snuff
Had driven by—
Then she went blind

And kept her route,
Drove an army surplus jeep,
Made cowboys tough
From long bull rides
Bounce like rabbits
Down in the ditch
As she swerved their way,
Slew-foot, pure blind, through—
Junior McKean took the keys away—
She said she'd stitch his badge
Right to his shirt with lead—
When Mildred died
They approached her grave
On the gumbo buttes of the south Star Route
"…To make damned sure
Her coffin ain't got tires,"
So Junior said—
As the bright wind blew his wet-combed hair,
He stroked the brim of his old felt hat
With both big red, chapped hands—

***

Blessed Eye

We found a priest that
Dressed in brown, some kind of bison hides?
It was cold rain in an empty park on a white November
    day—
His eyes and beard were grey—
The oaks were bare, planted pillars in between
The rows of spruce and pine—
He made us our vows in the late afternoon…
As the light leaned down on our children standing by;
Bride, groom and bare, wet ground,

The soggy rug of matted gold and yellow leaves—

When he spoke the riddle we call the "three in one",
My little girl, with two thick braids, cut loose and ran,
Leapt and cart wheeled on the grass until finally the
Priest and bride both laughed, released, aloud,
Beneath the low, now snow filmed late-breaking west-lit
    sky—

***

Important Dance

The wind roars at 40 mph from Northwest
As Camel John floats in at equal speed from south—
The sunlight comes in at speed of light, you know,
Sintered (Whitwho'dee?) further south, foil-like sheets of
    light—
The door of the schoolhouse faces north—
At 3 pm those doors slam open, stuck—
3rd graders first, and finally 5th,
Flood through the space out onto gravel,
Against the boom, the gusty wind,
Into blind-eyed solace, natural light,
And the leaves, as if they've been in wait,
Rise up tornados' welcome: yellow-gold—
They keep pace with each fast kid
In the most complex important dance,
That wind and sun, leaves and kids, will ever do—
As Camel John investigates, and hesitates,
He sees the tales of the winter prairie town—
"But from the God of the Burning Bush,
His deaf ears do not yet hear."

***

Basketball Hearts

They tell us this is some basketball
Town, ah hummm?
They say that a coach's heart
Broke down, and the whole town grew
Their Hearts the size of a pounding golden ball,
And the ball made a swoosh in the neat stringed nets
Like the sound blood makes as
It rushes in through heart' chambers, out again—
And in this town the basketball heart
Still beats so hard that you can't
Help but know the name of
The heart that made it so; that so?

And John Camel John knows the blade, the axe,
Cross roads of crosses, open graves—
We like to call this thing the innocent name: yes, History!

***

House Ghosts
(Ross, Nicole, Kyle, Linda and Dave)

There you were, you one or all:
At it again,
Long after occasional paperback
Books under beds
Or propping up the electric motor
Hooked to blower for the solar heat
Were cleaned up, read or gone;
Tennis rackets (still use them now),
Basketballs and footballs too,
87 fishing poles, all tangled, string to string—

These lonely sacred objects there,
Beneath the weight family days,
Delicate, tangled dreams—
We moved out the old sailor bunk,
Snuggled up into the corner, the northwest room,
To make some space for a
Hand-me-down to bed a queen-sized guest—
I found two softened playing cards,
Louisa May, the Alcott girl,
And Robert, Louise, Stevenson—
I caught them flagrant, worn, entwined
Beneath the mattress pad—
So unlike them both, the paper romance there—
I saved them both awhile—
Louisa sleeps in "The Abbot's Ghost",
And Robert leans, all lean and debonair,
Against his set of gilded works,
Fake or real leather bound
{Treasure troved on a reckless day:
The Department Chair
Decreed they all be thrown away}—
So now we have new thoughts of you
That make me think what we will leave?
Ghosts in another 40 years, at least,
I paganly pretend—
Remember the clearly laid-out prints
Of little hands and names
On the corner of the concrete backyard court?
There's a new and twin-trunked
Apple tree,
Planted from your apple seeds
4 feet high in the wild flower bed
And a gravestone,
Granite, grey,
For Tommy the Hermit Crab,

And another stone for the
Murdered rabbit (one or two, maybe cousin or some
    rabbits you all knew)
That the new boy found (stiff and dead, with a broken
    chest)
Beneath the Canadian Cherry
By the gravel walk
On the outer-Northwest wall—
Today I write my final will:
Boil my body down to bones
Reconnect my frame with wire,
Skull and all,
In the shape of a northern
Celtic cross—
Paint the crucifer
A yellow red, blue on black—
Chain it all to a metal pole
Strung with prayer wheels,
Ribbons, stones,
Shiny cans, polished tin
That flickers, blinding, blinding,
—Cottonwood leaves in wind—
Not so good I guess—
Not so subtle, natural,
Gracious, sweet—

Not like the children that you were; or are, somewhere; or
may be again—I will start planting pages of poems with
chicken bones—In nooks and corners, out in the old
compost pile— (Say—we found the bones of a long dead
mouse in the—Wall beside the sink in the sunroom
several years ago) I'll try for something graceful now,
More dingling pagan done, Play my cards right, Lay
handprints down, cunning, accidental—The way you did:
Apple trees, books and memories—Memories linger,

linger, linger. The way you do, Sweet and young as
Ancient, once new Irish Hymns

Birds and leaves out the window in the wind—
Leaves leap and fly down the street
And make me think they are yellow finches—
Purple leaves flip off trees and drop like the sparrows
In the very same tree,
And just to blind-side me some more—
Real sparrows come and go
Rising, dropping; leaf and sparrow,
Sparrow, yellow leaf, not finch,
And then again;
I am dizzy, drowned in beauty—
The Beloved teaches from so great a spatial distance—
Don't tell me the mystery—

{Camel John has studied his science, looped as he is in
the coils of the Hairy God: Desmond Morris, I have
become suspicious of you—When will the deaf ear hear
the pounding tom-tom of a Ringo-back-beat —Joy in
Rockapocylypso?}

Dogs, that cat, dolphins and one horse friend—Your
naked aggression motif pales—I read you like a King
James Bible then—Those last days of horny high school
genius—This morning, I watched two full-grown brown
sparrows—Brown for sure, by my late summer color
chart—Full grown, as I, pretty full—one sat in the
purple—Branches of the Canadian Cherry—The other
pecked seeds by the beak-full —From some short, dried
up, seeded-out-Bushy white and green grass on the
lawn—Then the sparrow flew up, sucked beaks with the
bird—In the purple leaves, again and again—And shared
some seeds—so, what do we make of this? Did you read

Darwin's other book? Naked apes aside, I would like you
to think—"When does the nature of dumb instinct—
Change to wondrous gene-driven holy wisdom?"*

From David Thoreau (attn. David Fuller)

***

Looking Fierce

Over the years
Many birds have flown
Into the windows on our balcony,
Deceived by seeming transparency:
Several sparrows,
Always known to be, well, flighty,
And grey or brown—
(One died of a broken neck)
One Mourning Dove,
Usually so full of dignity,
Cooing on the wires
Or gliding down the street
With that comforting feathered purr;
One yellow finch, a surprise,
With the way they always swoop,
Dive and streak,
Brave pilot's stunts,
Avian acrobats without wires;
And then the red tailed hawk—
He hit the glass so hard it
Should have shattered—
All those birds,
Intent on mistakenly flying in…
And me,
Intent on looking out—

Only the wild-eyed hawk looked back at me:
Frightened enough at what we saw,
We crouched before the glass,
Hunched down,
Ready to fight, look fierce!!

And so, well, Black Wolf,
We come back to you,
Off on the edge of the poplars in the snow—
Are you too wild to admit to Christmas?
I stand here freezing in this camel hide coat,
Neither cloaked or hidden from you, the cold,
Or God the bush on fire—
For all I know you are the three in one—the same—
With a web belt around my middle,
Grenades and clips all dangling down—
You! Too cagey? (bad word, cage)?
For the silence moves
Against and over the still white where color meets the
     snow-lit dark—
Is it a matter of the red berries, so pin sharp, tiny?
High bush cranberries dried there
Where the White Tails browse, can't reach—
I know you, out here,
You with my God blind eyes both closed,
And scent your deep hide smell—
My fingers stink from the sleek, hot musk,
The smooth oil of your winter pelt—
Lurk—or haunt (there, there's the better word)—
Haunt, hunt in the snow beneath the branch
Of white hooded druid pines—
We revel in the December moon, the Word—

You are blessed, black mother in dark light,
Even moonlight, star light, and the light that

Rises from the snow itself—they bless,
And I bless too, knowing you were there,
Knowing you would gnaw my bones
At the drop of our God's hand—
May you sleep in peace—
I know—you hear my dreams—

Cold December flies away at the rose red splendor
All the world lay under death
Eyes were closed in sleeping
But when all seemed lost in night
Came the sun whose golden light
Brings unending joy, brings the endless joy
Of our hope, highest hope,
Of our hope's bright dawning, sun beloved of heaven
—Catalonian Carol, Howard Hawhee, tr.

You are Learning a New Walk and More

{And we can guess by now that Camel John, Collector of
Broken Clocks, keeps his case notes in his head while he
tinkers the insides of the clocks and gets himself heavy,
holy, heedless, hooded, hopped-up on tea and sugar
cookies too—Heavy dreaming done, facedown on old
newspaper piles.

There is awareness, clarity of the itch on the palms and
feet like nail-holed healing or the hair follicles that grow
on the Wolf Man—How do I admit to these things? The
lurch in the Dianna-arrowed clarity of moon light, the
secret desires that only a public politician must admit in
public access hearings/Admission—after awareness,
which adds up to confession: step in the booth, put the
priest to sleep with detailed and predictable lust. Then

147

make a plan of action—the Hail Mary's of redemption plans, face the daily hurt of daily forgiveness and the resentment you need to feel before you admit that you need to be forgiven.

Back to the first step—look at your hairy, low-browed, flesh-eating face in the mirror- window to her room, the clear reflection of the moon in Diana's sparkling moon shine—see? Awareness, confession, apology, incarnation, affirmation, the caramel taste of incantation—need that is sweet and free from lust, and the affection that can exist once you know you have seen the object of carnal desire in the simple, apple crunching admiration—

I cannot number the steps—pull yourself in your hairy skin under the glass-eyed microscopic insight of moonlight, then up and on your journey where you scoot down the path on you diapered bottom, after which you crawl along on your hands and knees, and finally, he or she reaches down and lifts you up on two feet. Why? How? Because the Holy Wisdom of I AM roars from one body to another with the power of a moon-powered tide.

Celebrate your sleek coated hairy soul, angel beast. You now walk on two feet; hold paws with the flesh of the soul you desire, while you trade bits of the redeemed red apple. The Kingdom is at hand, you learn, and more...at hand, as in right now and always}

***

Once, this Time, Again Today

The Blue Jay from yesterday lurks
Like a flapping yahoo
In the branches of the ornamental
Oriental apple tree across the street—
One black sparrow, not black
Not dusty black, but silver dark, is not afraid at all—
He braves the loud guitars of jays
And pecks in the dirt of the
Still-blooming flowers of the wooden tub
While the other sparrows,
As silly as stock brokers, panic
Back into the branches of the
Canadian cherry tree—
This is amazing here beneath
The blank blue sky on
October first, pretending summer,
Two seconds from winter's windy bite—

Admit it now—
You see it with me
We could hold hands
And not be ironic—
Even that would be God's gift,
What we humans call
An accidental grace—

That is not a jay in the tree,
But two mourning doves
Cavorting like they
Think this is Palestine somewhere near 3 BC—
I will not look away—
Christmas can come—
The red berries stay

On the tree when the
Leaves are blown and gone:

Winged At Once

That laugh,
Chuckling across the river
Of sound into my hairy deaf ear
Makes me want to be 12 years old somewhere near 2 BC,
And be the boy that fell
In love with the laugh
So that now, years later,
Your laugh is a precise
Moment: past, present
And there you go again,
Your deep-throated sound
And then sexy and angel-
Winged all at one: future, tense!

***

And Again, South Past

That Canadian Cherry and the
The ornamental apple,
I find myself, looking, squinting,
"Discombobulated",
Says my mother's voice,
But the white brick house with red asbestos shingles
Still looks like a fine estate,
The tower and roof of the
Lutheran church in the valley
Becomes the Temple in Jerusalem—
The high school halfway

Up the south slope of the valley
Takes on the solid strength
Of a Hellenic gymnasium wall—

The squeaky white vinyl of
The new condos strung
Along a street up that hill
Is a chain of white house-dwellings—

The light!
Is it dust, the lower angle of sunlight?
The autumn tilt of the earth?
How does the yellow, gold-brown
And occasional red
In leaves and grass change the light?
Is it the dry sky, empty of rain?
I am lost in some Mediterranean scene—
If you were here,
You would see this, you see?
I go on writing to keep you near—
Sooner or later, maybe,
Something I say will
Capture the attention of your beauty—
How foolish of my words to say, "That is all I want. That
    is all."

(From the prayers of Camel John, Beaver Creek U, 2008 back to 2002)

{I am meeting with the bored and broken—Beings
binding this institution—Of Higher Philoso-Fire into a
meaningful Techtonic whole—Needless to say, I'd rather
be with you—Plato is a boor—

Open Letter to The Arts Academy Faculty of Beaver Creek: I found out, just last week, or so, that I was to be in four places at once. The ghosts of the old Hopi Medicine Man, Kurt Vonnegut Jr., Albert Einstein, and the Ragged and Raging Hebrew Prophet howling Outside the city walls of Old Jerusalem, all them surrounded me in a Cloud of holy witness and doom: and so I said, in tune with that—Strange quartet of fire-eaters, shamans and clowns, Saints of Time, "Everything that ever happened, ever will happen, and is happening Right Now will always be happening: 'World wit out end, Amen.'".

So I stayed at the lake, slept in on Monday, looked at the seagulls and—Buzzards, drank cappuccinos, chased my wife through the trees, And gazed at the endless lapping waves that used to be the world's Longest river: the wide, chocolate, cream kissed Old Dead Sea. Knowing that I would be caught, trapped in the 4 pronged fork of history, Detected (by Darrel, Lection of Duty, Howdy) by the Chair of our deportment, I wrote this letter, noted on stone tables, then jammed it in my pocket, Which then to my dismay, I stuck in the washer where it turned to fibers and clumps—That would be perfect for the nest of the Blue Jays that live next door: Baptisimo! I cannot avoid the water—I am, oh eggo ist Mir, am deaf to all but the spirit that —Descends in the form of the mourning dove! So now, I plead my case with you, paragons of present tense and recorders—Of the rhetoric of past and future, be not so intense, intention, yours and mine aside: If Einstein, Vonnegut, Hopi, and Hebrew have it connected right, I am still there writing this note, which you will, in the future, which—Soon becomes past, have read (although right here in the "be here now")—You cannot touch or see, you will, or did, and so for all the "eternal now"—With Heidegger (I Digress, too much admired in

my degrees, Mister of Divinity, Candy Maker Preacher),
and miss that fact that I am not there, for now—But find
a way to forgive my experiments in The Physics of the
Liberal Arts—And know…All passive sins of the past
projected as guilt in the—Present aside, that forgiven, and
shriven, I will again, among you be—The next time and
tide and tea and rabbit call us all to meet, Lewis,
Meriwether, C.S. and Carroll, unworthy though I am,
Mystrificated by Doves and Water—

At the great meeting room in the eternal Hall of Then,
Now and Next—Amen.}

***

Camel John Turns Purple in Your Shirt—

I have learned that the ornamental apple tree
Across the street in my Niebuhr's yard
Is the original tree of the knowledge of good and evil—
Now you need to know this—
The serpent was too wise "fore {skin} his own
    seersuckers pants"
And alligator boots!
YOU will not die— Yah, right—Yew Bet—said the druid
So he bite the little bitter red apple
And pretended to like,
Actually did like it, just to get you to bite it too,
Because he was already bitter himself: a life of sales,
And too many years and fears for the MBA in
Deathlehem Graduate School—

Eve bit it, gagged and gulped,
Decided: Adam, that ass! She
Decided to give him the bite as well—rib to rib—

153

And so it went, these mythic eras,
Mmmm, about, as, long, until
Our wandering mother/father,
Red Clay, scoria-gumbo,
Wandered back to North Dakota: Here
And now you know:
Showing your beauty is not lust—
It is not gynecology, genie or genealogy—
It is wisdom, dangerous, dark—
Most of us just don't get the feel—
Look across the street—
The apples gleam in the morning
After a cold day of rain, wind, and light snow

(Old Tom Fool we miss you too,
With the glass apple on your desk and
World apple in your holy poems)—
So some beauty is not to be touched
Or bitten,
But looked at, loved in this moment—
Don't tell me this ain't no mystery—
Prairie flowers grow in shit!
You would turn Camel John Purple with your
Philoso-fie and bile-shit—And Your Beauty?

…As pure as your purple cone flower—Purple in the shit
of the endlessly rollicking grasslands that grow it—An
holy hand, writ on de wall of de Empire's holy
temple/tempter/temp = Redemption < New!!!!
Recreation < Growth index, Restoration < Cancer is a
growth—With no respect for Marx or the ilk of Adam
Smith, I defer to Eve!

Classics: Romeo and Juliet, 20 Years On

Her body, she vehemently won't admit, is still the one after nearly two decades with the same man, including the lack of stretch-marks from a baby. Her body stretched thin, taut, wire-tight muscle—the runner, or the archer maybe—she cannot sleep. He is on his stomach breathing like a full groaning dog and letting enormous farts. Every few minutes he snores, groans and farts— loudly—then groans again. She moans, poetically, gently, and quietly. The room is dark, no next-door lights in the window; the yard behind their back yard is dark too. It is always dark up there, unless the single man with two dogs and the occasional girl friend is in the hot tub.

Finally she gets up and floats, half hallucinating, upstairs to the living room, to evade her living groom, nests on the couch, lowers the largest window blind enough to cut off the glare of the streetlight and wraps herself in a blanket. Suddenly he is there above her, hovering, lurching, beside her: "You go back to bed; I'm keeping you awake."

She sits, holds the blanket around her: "No."

He says, "Go. You have to get up, but I get up later."

She sighs, disgusted, and goes.

He sits in the dark and watches the trees toss in the wind; He wonders about where those "tossing" words came from—the trees aren't tossing; the branches are waving back and forth. She is tossed. He will toss. The metaphor fits them and the waving tree branches. It will snow any day, and then dead turkeys and another Christmas.

"Waving back and forth," he thinks, then pictures her like a tree, leaning left, right, bending, rising up straight (her perfect posture). He wonders how tired she gets of basic, untutored, biological male behavior. She farts too, but quietly, never stirring, little, sweet bubble strings of gas. The hair on his stomach makes her happy. She still hides her nakedness, and he still spends time trying to catch her.

She has always protected her private skin like a nun; he, far too old for the job, continues to act like a 12-year-old pervert. He thinks she is asleep. There are shadows against the living room window. ...Shadows, tossing in the strong wind.... He thinks he will sleep and does, and here is what would have happened to Romeo and Juliet if they had lived longer.

***

You Know You: Now

The sparrows are back in the purple leaves
Of the Canadian Cherry—
After a Sunday of wind and spraying rain,
After a Monday of Northwest wind and
A lowered autumn sun
The tiny apples in the tree across the street
Are looking dull
And will remain that way
Until the leaves are blown down
And rain or ice or snow
Polish the marble sized fruit

So they shine like holly berries—
In the middle of a song,
I stop—the air is suddenly still—
The sparrows all disappear—
Coming back to me…
Just down the street,
First in the long shadows,
Then in the long spears
Of saffron sintered sunlight: October—
The beloved one is walking—
She has been away—

She has never been gone
Or ever been here, for sure,
And she returns, from nowhere,
Where no verb tense will function now—

No one woman,
A certain lady,
She moves from shadow to light,
Light to shadow—
She strolls on the summit of the hill:
Past the gymnasium and the philosophers and their boys,
The Temple and the locked gates of the Fortress on the
    Hill
(But you know all this by now)—
She stops at the low-walled
South-leaning dark wooden house
Built to face into the sun, dug
Into the southern side of a northern hill—
You know you now: October is shot—
Little darling, it's been a long, cold lonely winter.

***

Letter to Editor
NYTBR   RE—Unsafe at Any Read
10/19/08

Great Literature once found me, the midst of—The steel-
cold winter troubles of youth—Icy sidewalks of snow-
paved plains. But Wordsworth worked me there— And
handed me the "Spots of Time". Hemingway, Cohen,
Yuri Yevtushenko and Ferlingetti—Danced so deep in
my blood-conscious joy: Just words, the sounds of
wonder in words.

Underground, in dark nights—Writing notes on the
lignite veins of my soul (I swear my teeth are yellow from
lignite-stained,   soft   prairie   water)—The   sound   of
words—Old Bobby Z, John, Paul, George and Ringo—
caught me, before the booze—The guidance counselor or
a preacher's doom—And said, "Decide, each day, then;
then, again"—

And before Harold Bloomed and Leopold blossomed, I
learned to be alone there with my {S} elves—Dear
Tolkien, before Orlando Bloom moved Middle Earth to
New Zealand. Joyce had a voice that left no choice—
Molly had to Bloom! And when I met the girl of my
dreams—She loved me for the sound of my words—
When Saul Bellow sat ("...sit at the typewriter,")—He
opened my heart to and I "Sized up the Day"—Where I
learned the Beatles and Handel by, Ooh dat water music's
sweet!

By heart, so nada, Rubber Soul, my own—Revolver,
Sergeant Pepper, Boho-beat and all—There on the icy
banks of the North Dakota Ocean, I Scaled the

sociological prairies of the—Social register twice—And avoided the banker's daughter. Great Literature saved my very life! With only the lightest irony, Dear Siegel, I say with Evangelical literal lyrical joy, Literature Saved Your Life! And got you a Job at the New York Times.

***

Election: 2008

I am walking in the Sacred Grove,
And so must not have hours—
Here today on this odd day of late
December, the titmice chitter and
The grey squirrels are at it,
Debating creation with the brave
Prairie crows that stayed last fall,
These last days before the
Coronation, and Fall
Of our newly elected King,
Who rumor has is an African lord—
News folks he say will take
His oath on Abraham Lincoln's bible,
And you, me, and Abraham at least
Know what that means—
The trees are empty, and
Their bark is tight and dry,
But the air is blue and as clear
As my true love's eyes in time—

Blue Angel's BLUE JESUS: RISING!

***

The ancient Irish passed on to us the
Holly wreath, the garland and mistletoe—
We are mostly peasants with presents
Beneath our tree—
Here's my ten-year-old boy on bad timing:
I say, "That was bad timing."
He says, "That's ok. Bad timing happens
Thousands of times a day;
Don't you think millions?
Even around the world?"
I say, "I do. I think so, I do." And peasants with presents
And German Lutherzen Odin trees
And Druidic holly and mistletoe
Gather around the icy steel
Inside the barns and tables…
And wait for the Judean peasant king,
Judah, The Lion—Bob Marley is welcome here!
Which time was bad timing?
This Christmas, last Christmas,
Or 2000 years ago in Ramah?
That Sinai God, reformed from
Fire, flood and tempestuous jazz Job jobs,
Abandoning ark and some would claim,
Ark of the Covenant and a Temple too, in the arc
Of the Gospel According to
Poor misunderstood Isaiah
And Indiana Jones as well—Heil!

Or has it happened, this
Rule of Heaven among us,
Poorly translated,
Not by God, but by
Gospels in Greek and
Popes and Priests and

Karl Marx and the Smiths, Joseph and Adam his older
    brother?

What is it, here, among us,
Lurking where only
WB Yeats, in his regret,
And Tough Shit Eliot,
In his vengeance, can see it—
Indeed, who knows?
Poppa John Knows—
Camel John Knows—
No Horse Erdrich
And Mad Blue Star Mac WRATH know it too—
Bob Dylan,
"I know and you know, that
I know and you know!!!!"
I once more proclaim the
Blue Star on the "global warming"
The proper and proposed time of "climate change",
(I believe, but can't we find the better phrase of
    catastrophe?)
Blue Horizon,
Here in the "…Ice Box Of The North", Eh? Whit Woe,
    Wisdom?
Out there, Poppa John,
West of Manhattan, Beyond the Bedroom Wall(s),
Where James Town calls and the little badlands roll
Away in the lonely rear-view Lear!

***

Camel John's Shoveling Song

I'll burn hot a shovelin' snow
I'll burn down to burnin' coals

Then in the bucket, out I'll go
Dump my ashes to melt some snow!!!

*Memory's aim is to be there, leap the present, persuade us the past is
identical to the future, prophetic, our one seat of reference—those
blank spaces we slip from to find we've been suspended in the past.
That suspension is memory's power; memory is imagination.*
—Larry Woiwode, What I think I Did

***

Blue Jesus: Rising!

Read and said out loud
Comes Camel John Haraldsen
Into the bully pulpit—
Sent from the hot sands of
Palestinian madness
To the white ice sands
Of the Dakotan dunes on the high plains
For a break down processional cantata—
Pep talk, my boy!
Just short of preacher:
Tall tale, no tell 'em all Shekinah Whirlwind secrets—
Parables come after preambles,
But these, the unattached, unmoored wisdom teachings
(No Gnostic or pragmatist or Bookkeeper to keep them
    kept!
Praise the Burning Bush!)
Pronouncements of Word—John, waggle 'em proudly!
No Jordan River, no Jerusalem, Slim,
Just old Camel John Locust man,
Proudly wounded, Haraldsen of the old Hot Wind
On Dry Grass that withers and fades as the flower,
Proudly proclaimed in wild honey wonder—
I Come To Bail Out The Little Boat—
Let us Raid the Ruins of Knowledge, Law, and any
Gospel set out in grids and straight and narrow lines!
(And other such modern human failings)
In long and SHORT! In longing I come as an old hairy
    boy,
This midnight vigil of your Mid-Advent years—
With these spouted words of wisdom in hand,
Just the far side of a poem, with no (I tongue my cheek)
    metaphor,

I swear that, and true, you believe it,
And after that I will sell you a desert city for sure—
I have learned to talk from the forked tip
Of the ever-present tempter's tongue —
Same little devil tried to get Jesus
To Shaman leap from the tit of the temple
And turn stones to bread for snakes—
If these spouts of whale belly brine and power
Redeem your 21st century brain to the bowels and deeper
Down to the place where weeping and guts meet SOUL,
EVEN RUBBER SOUL will do:
"In the beginning, I misunderstood.
But now I've got it—the Word is Good!"
(Lennon, not the commie, but John, Not the Baptist,
But just that mop-topped cowboy Beatle, martyred, never
        gone)
Win or lose, I give up and go back to the King—
In fact I will, if you can't hear his song in this poem
(Who ever said it wasn't a poem)—Lo, How Leopold is
        Blooming!
I'll have Molly B. singing, half in rut, Irish Rose, any
        day!!!!
Better a belted blues from a horny-eyed Irish Girl
Than a sermon from an angry agnostic Jewish Saint
(Who just refuses to Curse God and Die).

1

So SAY NO MORE of

The Canadian Cherry, cheery in summer,
Empty now of birds and leaves
After the ice storm (it was meant to be you see)
And snow in November (give thanks in death)—

No tell me-no tell me-tell me never a no!
The webworm pods all looked like birds
In the sunlit, ice sheathed silver-grey branches:
Them are worm pods (not cocoons my lad)—
Butterfly comes from a cocoon—
Tree killer worms eat the wood when they
Hatch from the ugly black pods—

Look at the empty birdhouse hung there,
The ghost of past Christmas gifts,
In the center crotch of bole and branch—
Would you make one autumn moment, a memory
Scribbled on paper, some kind of Biblical
Wisdom and a farce all at once? (It is!)
Say no more; say no more, the British comedian said
(He was Camel John's 2nd cousin, my lad)—
The Gospel comes, needs it to be,
Even on BBC reruns from 1973—

2

Londuinn Frigg im Ancient Saxonic stutter; Latino
Beatle boots on the cobbles of Liverpool-Jerusalem-New
      York!
Here's your Friday-Sunday December wisdom—
They said that the snow and wind
Would come on Saturday, Saturn's Day,
The Dead End across the frozen river day—
But it comes on Fryda's day instead—
Now, is the time—where is the refrain?
I need a pop tune to pull me true!
Here is the hidden consonantal code:
Not YWH, but, instead,
The alphabet of stable [poop] and grace!

I-ego Eimi and me and thee
B-for Beatrice (remember old Dante?
Well, he was I, young lad, Old Camel John was Dante)
C-Candydydicica, black wolf Celt, mother of whelps,
    poetess of souls
J- for Jazz, Sophia light strummed strings of ice and fire, a
    wooden guitar,
And a voice that says, "Come to Bethlehem and see..."
    Blue!
And H—Lady Hawk, Beauty, lover to beast, bird by
    night,
Woman in day light, far out ahead of herself and us all—
This is the vision of Camel Hide Dante Haraldsen
Take it, or eat it—wild honey is pure old girl!

3

John Brings Yeats to Springfield Avenue
(for Brendon)

On Friday, a grey morning after the first great snow
    storm
In 3 years or 7,
He is out back piling the snow and rolling like a dog—
With each new flight of geese from northwest to
    southeast,
Comes the child's oracle voice through the kitchen wall
(Not the bedroom wall this time, Whit Hoot Wide word,
    Wise bird)—
"Dad; Dad! Look, look and see"
V after V past my counting—
On Saturday afternoon, out in the back with him,
I dig snow blocks for his hilltop fortress—

He does the stacks, and shapes, pats, patches and
    sculpts—
I dig down deeper: sin-fishing Liberal Arts Reject,
    Adjunct,
Special contract word mongering deaf man of melody for
    HIRE:
ME! At 4:30, late in the afternoon for them,
The orange candle tips of the sun spear and spread to
A sheet of thin hammered roseate foil up, over
And across our sky, southwest and into the advent blue
And black of the northeastern Canadian air—
"Look to the east", I shout to him, so loudly he jumps,
And we stand and see more than half the moon stand out
Of the light in the north—"Look to the East!"
Then we see the snow geese, not more than 50,
Fly in single file across the face of the moon—
{Save me from Meta foraying psycho Freud,
That adolescent wants a man to be a god attempt
Too hallow the all too venial human drive—
Save me from Theo OLOGY,
The ancient human scheming sin
That chains the mystery of it all to a doctrine wall—
Boy: I give you Camel John right now—
Bless me my son, so I may bless you in turn.}

Of course, I don't say those words—
Wings of geese sing in chorus
Above the burial grounds of the
Indian holy ones and the ancient rocks—
There are Blue Angel eagle eyes in the sky above us son,
And they see the Kingdom Come,
Not trapped by time lines and lies of angles[*]
He says, "I hope their droppings don't fall

---

[*] My rude word love copped from my other older poem

167

On me," and some laughter follows,
Forced poop smell on my pious lines—
Then we go back to work on the new
Hill fort at hand—

*Educated people run on rationality until they encounter a situation
beyond their control, an accident, a troubling situation with a
daughter or son—and then give it up or change enough to realize
that rationality isn't necessarily the engine running the universe.*
—Larry Woiwode, Acts—

4

Camel John's Warning

Feel a big sin trip coming down little, er, mister or miss?
Is it a nice day for a Rockapocylypso?
(He quotes St. Stephan O' Files the fellow Cajun martyr.)
"You wanna be anorexic, little twit?" he bellows,
"You ain't Mary, old Let It Be, Mary,
Tough little 'Amen' said-to-the-angel Mary—
You'd starve yourself on the stable blues
And sneak off to the porcelain confessional
In the midst of a Christmas feast—
If God fathered a God on you,
You'd hold your arms out to look skinny
In all the Italian paintings,
And we'd call you the Madonna
Of anorexic bones—
Baby god would have to suck on
Stable cow milk—
You'd be dry as a
Mannequin's Manichean plastic tit!"

Oh, look out little twig of a girl!
Old Camel John,
Smelly, honey!
Succulent spirit!
Crazed up, raised up John Haraldsen says—
"Let me hold you down, girl,
In that clear winter spring
By the thundering rocks
By the big smoking river—
Until you scream, SWEET BABY JESUS!
BLUE JESUS RISE UP IN ME!
And Shekinah mamma washes
Your phony, evangelical church school fashion model
Milk-skinned blues away, away from YOU."

Old Camel John Haraldsen, son of Herald the dust land
      farmer—
I'm hunger-I'm thirst-I've lived on the farts of my own
      devil's breath,
That same little bugger that tempted Jesus to serve him
      and
Got hard beans of judgment shoved down his gut for a
      good times blow—
"Girl, you sin hunter, wanna die babe, barely big enough
      to
Dream the dirty boogie with no body fluids or sperm!
You could be free if I can keep you from choking on
      bread and wine!
I wrap you in camel, poor honey drenched locust down
Your hunger throat
Until you no longer choke on the Bread of these words:
I FEAR LOVE AND TRUST—I FEAR LOVE AND
      TRUST—
You are one girl on the edge of the Great Prime
      Mobile—

God Knows, when Camel John gets called out on you like
The last dark hound of heaven;
God knows, "it won't kill you—it ain't poison", (Says Bobby D)
Said, "youuuurrrr gonna seeeervvv some bodeeeee…"

5

You do, you mean you, all American Voodoo Credit Union Kittie?
Drive with Camel Skin John—what center-line-turning lane?
There ain't no middle of the road no more!
"People Keep Comin," old Blind Willie sings,
"But the Train is GONE!!!"
It's a one-way trail out here—see the snow all piled in stacks
Of white frozen dung in a meat locker Norksy vision of hell?
Git out yer SUV and drive hot ice on the one lane highway out of Hell—
White, white man, old boom busted, wheat king bonanza middle of the
Geo-political center of a happy rich hell on earth,
Where they don't even know the difference—
This nuclear winter wonderland where we guard the bones
Of dead democracy, stock broker, trust fund sons to
Farmers that made it rich sellin' wheat to the Chinese Commies!
Where you be turning to for wisdom now, stealing some Joy juice now?

America's Anchorman, fat-chinned-failed at college,
    never
Held a job or read a real book, limbo rolling liar Rush't to
    hell and gone?
Or FOX news—not the wise old red or Ojibwa named
    Grey Fox—
I mean the right wing burn the commie liberal extremist
    goof ball channel—
Set to rile the O'Reilly's all the way back to the green
    shores of potato land?
Who do you listen to, Missy?   Get your news from deaf
    old John—
Only thing I hear comes straight from the burning roar
    and fire of God—
Open the Prophet's Mouth—out spews the river
    Jordan—
It is 20 below in the northern plains, and we been left for
    dead!
Hell can be freezing, and that's the reason for the
    XMASS season!

6

Old John comes out, a silent dangerous place in the hole
    shot in my heart—
Between Christmas and New Years Eve, 3 am,
    Bradbury/Woiwode time,
Them red rod red rued deviled up scoria bad lands
Where I found no drink, no water, nor even an ice cold
    beer—
And Johnny, go Johnny Go, comes jamming, a Hendrix,
    Norterno Man,
Haraldsen from the Frisian lands, Celt with the Gospel
    on his tongue,

His tongue on the strings of a burning black growling
    Gretsch guitar—
He takes me down to wash again,
Old camel blues Johnny,
Honey locust John,
Wild honey from the bees in rocks
Where the muddy water
Runs until it is clear as the Jabbock,
As clear as the jabberwocky rocks,
Oh Lewis, the other, Carroll, you
Mad word loving (Dylan Thomas, Paul Simon says he
    was)
Camel John lover just for the sound of words, you!
From hell to "Put the fires out!"
Where Lucy and the lion take
Their stand on the bridge,
Backed up by weak-kneed needy me,
And the shy mad Oxford Don,
CS, and behind him the rag tag
Readers of bibles and children's tales—
The little girl, Lucy, pulls out
The silver dagger and the bottle of healing oil—
The Great Gold Lion roars in song,
And behind, in the madcap dance
Comes Honey John Haraldsen
Full of the jumpy, Locust honey Shine—
He flails about with his leather belt
While he dances and sings between; swings the black axe
    guitar,
The leaps of his locust Zen trained legs—
He tucks in his waist length beard,
Wipes blood and water from his gnarly hands
And stands in the water with Lucy and the Lion
While the hordes of human hatred howl,
And Hell's own bat winged bells beat down, he sings

The ancient desert father and mother blues—
He laughs like Sarah back in her tent:
"I live on the wind and air!
I piss on the snakes of Satan's blasted earth!
A Word is more real; I have placed the sandals on his
    calloused feet;
I dance for the Lord, Wisdom Lady Love, The Lion and
    Lucy too!"
He holds down the legions of Satan and man,
Head ducked, immersed and baptized deep
In water that fills the devil's guts with fire—
And he shouts out better than any sweet Black
Preacher ever sang it in his dreams—
"Who are you? You human fools,
You devil's spawn of the devil's dong?
Say you can't be saved with no salvation?
No God but a crust of bread and wine?
A stripling nailed and stuck on a stick of wood?
Down you go, you lost demonic lads —
You are not the ones to have the say that
You still cannot be saved.
Shut up, drown, and go down to my song,
And rise up in the NAME OF NAMES—
Shatter you horned king's hot ice blue smoked hell!
Rise up in the name of Eve, St Lucy,
In the NAME OF THE LION!"
And Camel John comes down on them
In a great wall of water that ain't been seen
Since the holy green of Canaan, Donegal, Friesian
Rose from the Northern Sea!!!!"

7

And they do, from Hibbing and Duluth to Merry Drab
    Liverpool too—
It's a Rock apocylypso—Hendrix Buddy, Holly berry blue
    guitar—
Oh, someone sings, "I know you'd like the back of my
    hand;
How bout the flat of my hand or so"
Its camouflage in the charnel house of American
    nightmare time—
Or Camouflage in the catacombs of Grey white
    Amirichkat graves,
In the immoral golden gravy train of mad mortality
    blues—
Beat back, back beat Ringo drums in Babylon (Bob
    Marley waits in the wings)

What else could the Lion and Little Girl do?
What if you woke up one morning in a fantasy gone
    wrong,
In which the sweet human values found in real work,
Sexual love and family, friendship, music, dance and
    politics,
Religious ritual, the breath of life itself, all these things—
You find them all replaced by a room with a couch, cell
    phone,
Video game system, iPod and a 72" flat screen digi mon
    blue window?
POP!! It's time for the unleashed dream—

Kingdom come in the place and a way the Babylon Cops
the least suspect—The guys that pay their salary, the grey-
faced kings of bankbook swing—Bull and bear, puts and
calls, futures and options and fake adoptions—The roots

of all our abominations that we dare not see—inside the vault of value—The monastic order of money, the growling goon of gelder—Gold in all its guises!!! POP—it's time for the unleashed beat—Here comes the mystical cowboy hero, the un—bought off, unburdened horse-lover—Widow and orphan sunset riding bandito of the dream, Buffalo buddy, sodbuster friend, and Native American field hand of far-flung prairie—Plain and tall—What's he twirling Bob? Why, Camel John, old Shane Wayne Ranger is twirling a—Halley's Comet, Mark Twain, words for the sheer made joy of joy lasso—Lasssooooo!

POP—he pulls the noose on the devil's horns, solid red and white and blinking Blue—pulls the noose on the devil's horns, times own prickly crown of thorns, And BAM! It's 1966 somewhere in a hideaway NYC or else LA—New City of Angels—Out by the swimming pool—a great chlorinated St John Camel-Skin of a baptitso Cool blue pool—

A Ballad—"Twirling Lasso", or "Sweetheart (who is) the Roping Fool, Twirls the Kingdom" (home for you and me to see for sure is here: now; not in Timmy Leary's Severed head)

4/4 Time, Ringo back beat solid—four chord—1/3/4/5—key of C—on verses—4/5 chord on chorus—while the bridge, written by George alone, holds the 3 chord for all four lines while the famous mop top harmonies build up above Paul's bouncing base into a 5 chord in the 7th as in GGGGGGG7—hold it and them chimes, walls of guitars, One mad Gretsch lead, three black Gibson J-40 bell ring out in acoustic, and Billie the Preston taking' home that Gospel tone on a boom big old

two board Hammond O big B 3, bigger'n than a B 52 in
heat—

Dylan, John and Paul and George were at the chapel in
    LA,
Strumming strings and singing tunes by Berry, Ravin' on
    Old Ray
Camel John remembers
He got the sessions down on tape
Chorus—
Twirl them lassos, on the strings,
Above the endless western light
The eagle flies, to that backbeat of love

Three guitars three ringing tones, bass bounce summer
    night,
Fingers, strings, and forgotten words: the sound came
    out just right
Out there in the deep blue pool, the Baptist heard the
    ancient hymns
Chorus—
Twirling right hands, slide on the strings,
Paul's hand on the left, back beat in the western night
The Lion in the hidden hills sleeps beside the little girl

Bridge

Spirit never breaks a trust
Faithfulness creates Her love
In the desert angels pray
In the Word the beauty never fades away

Guitars humming all night long, out above the fort
They sang the ancient holy Sun back down to planet earth

"Wheels and fires", Dylan sings, "its all wheels," sings
      John
George sings, here! "Here comes the sun", and Paul yells,
      "Let 'em in!"
(Bridge into infinity—backtracked voices and guitars}—
Spirit never breaks a trust
Faithfulness creates her love
In the garden angels pray
In the Word
Beauty never fades away
(And the song continues as we all fade away to blue)

8

Old Camel Jock John,
Hairy, wet John Haraldsen, is
Trapped in my true love's deep green chair,
A Santa blanket around his white shoulder bones—
The hot honey brandy calms him down from lost allegory
      dreams—
Hot honey brandy in his hands, hands grained, olive
      wood crossbars,
And he sighs and says, the tear off an true Irish-Jew,
      Cree-like in his eye,
"I'm back; I'm back where I don't want to be, but at least
      I got here."
I snort, drink in the Christmas lights and say,
"Well at least enjoy this fire;
We burn all apple wood this year
Trimmed from branches
Bearing fruit the year before...
"Before?" he growls, "I have had before and afters, and
      now is now
In Kingdom Come— I die and live for this my boy.

I been out on the cold West River roads, far north of
    Bethlehem—
A poor man lived on apples, in frozen fear and faith—
Pour on the brandy, honey son—I have heard the ice, a
    locust buzz
In my Cree-Judean bones—"
I say to John, "I'm sleep deprived"
He says, "You're sleep depraved,
And a dirty little habit, too—
You sleep too much, and that's the thing—
Attention for 2000 years."
"I'm constipated sorrow," I say
John says, "Eat some locusts, figs and pray
Hairy God will pry you loose—
An Old Oxford Don once said to me,
'You wouldn't pray if God hadn't heard you first—'
stuttered turds of words, I pray."
"I don't want a pilgrimage," I say to John,
"I want a couch, a TV Screen."
He shouts—his voice is stereo:
"Extremity in pilgrimage, you'll be made, a fat white
    boy—
On missions from your God, lost in the Dante-esque flat
    screen.
Christ a Mighty, I mean,
There ain't no TV's in that stable—"
I say, "Do you hear?" "Do I hear what?" He shouts.
"I prophet see deaf as a post—
Even you can't be no deeper deaf than John—"
"Why can't I hear?" I shout—
He bellows in my head: "We all hear what we want,
And from HE, the SHE or It, or what, God knows
Whether we want to hear or not,
But you will hear just what you need and what you don't
    want,

Which 'art' what that Word always does when it really
    roars:
What you call literal: is lateral, flatter than the plains,
(They ain't, the plains, that flat, at all—just walk'em, fat
    boy, walk—)"
"I don't know, just what I hear," I say,
And then get brave for my own Ghost:
"See, I had a phone call,
The last Christmas day but one,
A Sunday afternoon,
And my friend from New York, Brooklyn Heights,
Who taught me this guitar,
Takes the stab and says, to me,
"What are you doing now?
Shoveling snow or saving souls?"
At the butt end of the turkey,
When the buttered brandy's gone,
"What's a soul to say?" I say to John.
John guffaws his brandy down
And holds out his cup for more:
"You say it true," he says—
"I will do my 40 years of shoveling the snow.
That's enough, a simple role—
Let it be God who saves the souls!"
John says, "That which we thought was fear
Has changed to fearful fast—"
I say; "I live this hunger—fear—
How long the speed of hunger lasts."
Haraldsen shrugs his skinny shoulders,
Drinks down the honey-amber fuel:
"2000 years—I lost my head, to Herod's politic-kin'
    Cock,
Went all deaf in my attempts not to hear the Big Bush
    burn,

179

All a drip, a drop, a bucket there beneath that wet blue
    star—
Look, there, in the northern winter sky!
See the light? Time is not the speed of light—
There, Fat Boy, you'll need the best,
The telescope of God's own grand design,
God's own speed and time—
You move through your little days—
A locust dipped in wild honey moves along so very
    slow—
Go freeze out in the barn again some Christmas night—
You'll hear the Angel Army
That sings against all human noise—
I hear 'em here, my holy fingers stuffed deep in my waxy
    ears—
I've seen 'em in a nearly empty barn,
A pup, two sheep, a cow—
Them angels sing sharp as the frost—
Frost glitters on the rails of the stanchions of a cold
    winter barn—
They glitter and then sing:
"Ice and heat, blue angel, ice and fire, and iron on your
    tongue!"

Blue Angel: Rising

1

She and I bought a blue straw
Angel in a bargain mall one fall,
Imported from the Philippines,
Made of stiff, bent straws—
Her cone-shaped skirt was
Wrapped around a cardboard cone—

And now she's been here 16 years
To top our ragged trees—
She's the little peasant god, a promised hope,
A dream on the odd blue Kachina tree,
And she seems to sing these 4th world hipster blues—
Or Ragg-na-rocker Angel girl for all I know,
Little Sister to Blue Jesus, auntie to old John himself—

With blue- green lights, and years of decoration junk,
(We'd had that bell for 60 years, so Grandma Helen said,
It's all the way from-Frisian, Prussian, Irish, Scotland,
      Cree land—
Still she speaks, her voice, five Advents past her death—
Some as new as this one twisted, white, pipe cleaner,
      snowflake star,
The art of my son's hands)—
Or made from China,
Some from children that are no longer here—
(—Jesse Dylan, Stem of Staff,
Gift of Grace, Sea Byrd child,
Where was your Christmas spent this year?)
All hung on the odd, spread branches,
A very ragged peasant of a tree—

Here I sit on lowly plains
On a midnight clear,
The lights of Bethlehem, Bone Town,
Angeleos, David's not so royal town and Blue Jerusalem:
The lights across the hills below in
Long blue shadowed snow—
Redemption of the generations,
Wandering peasant's dreams,
Hopes and fears of all the refugees, and me.

2

Prussia, blue; Sweden, glass; Norway—the ancient farm
on the edge of the deep cut fjord; Ireland—green in the
garland, holly, berries, drunk with joy in the midnight,
hungry and dry by the next day: Oh, Donegal will we see
you again that Day—fergive the demmed Brits—fergive
them popes—fergive the potato and all—fergive them
Vikings too, and the Irish kings that got lost in their
myths; fergive the Canooks and Army boys fer all the
Cree and Louie the Priest and all the old buffalo…

I am praying with the Grandfathers—
I am singing with the Grandmothers—
That prayer re-makes my bones-
Rise up now old broken bones—buff-skinned, Gaelic
    drums, and Lamb of such
Great price-short grass, years, 10,000 miles,
Long drum and fiddle tune—now on one old black
    guitar—
All you Grandpas, Grandmas, you;
One in Kingdom Come;
I call your vision now—

3

There she is—Beauty wakes: you sleep—
She rides the top of the dry green tree,
Blue-grass woven—classic head,
Long hair pulled back,
Straight shoulders, "v" shaped back,
Small breasts, thin waist,
Long skirts around the legs that ride the tree—
How can I not still think who she might be?

One small bit of you just might be her?
Slender and merciful, young peasant angel,
She sings the blue Blue Jesus blues:
From stable, cross, from tomb to throne and truth—
Her wings, a gift from a red-tailed hawk,
Not soft angelic white,
But hawk harped wild, latticed blue,
That will launch her from this holy tree—
Is the midnight cold but clear?
All you Dead, more alive than we,
One in Kingdom Come, come now:
"Then took he him up in his arms,
Blessed God and said,
Lord now let you servant
Depart in peace, according to your word:
For mine eyes have seen salvation spoke,
Salvation which you have made real before
The people came;
A Gentile light in the pagan night,
And the glory of the fire oh Israel."

***

I would like a great lake of beer for the King of Kings:
I would like the people in heaven to be drinking
It through time eternal
—St. Brigit of Ireland (450-525 AD)

And all the while in backbeat, bobbing to the tune,
Ringo smacks the tom tom right,
A Back Beat only God can give, and
These days, John and George both gone,
Ringo sings on a newer song,

What are we doing, shoveling snow or saving souls?
I am shoveling snow until I rise,
Blue Jesus rising blues
I shovel snow instead of coal
Let the devil shovel coal
Let Blue Jesus save the souls

Then Herod, when he saw that he was mocked of the wise men, was exceedingly wroth, and sent forth, and slew all the children that was in Bethlehem, and in all the coasts thereof...
—St Matthew

Where this began as a roaring fire in a Christmas house, a house that seems built for Christmas, a dream with dreamers beside a fire, now, it ends, and always where it must for now, ashes, real ashes in the wood stove, on the day naming Jesus as the Christ, Simeon's vision of light. Hamas is shooting rockets into Israel. Israel is bombing Gaza, and moving in the tanks and mechanized infantry. Half the casualties are civilians, many of them children.

In the U.S. we wait to see if the wise son of a Moslem and girl from the state that gave us Oz can convince us to save us from ourselves. In a country some call a "Christian Nation", we might remember that Jesus says the Great I AM can make children of Israel from stones.

I live in a community that taught me faith in the conviction that the Kingdom is among us, has been for almost 2000 years. This means more than a coming in a Second Coming, more than a space of holiness within each us. My people believe in the "Kingdom among us..." between, cosmic glue, tougher than time, and faster than the speed of light. This Kingdom connects all things, forms all places and times, as we say, "One God, world without end, Amen." I end here, waiting—Yet I know that the thing we await is all around us, not as metaphor but as a reality: among us.

I wait for all the poems of promise To become real—Not a New Heaven and Earth, But the old restored, redeemed as promised, So real and fresh with Eden's dew that It seems to be a new creation—I plan to see all of you, Lucy, The Lion, and all the other characters there, certainly Camel John Haraldsen, as real as me.

So one final dedication: to the children and descendants of all the peasants that suffer while they wait for the coming of the real King; and dear God have mercy on all the Children of Herod's fear and rage, here and everywhere else—
—New Years Eve, 2008, Last Day of Christmas, January 5, 2009, Epiphany, 2009

...Spare me! —All life a step toward death under the lintel of heaven's gate, my father and others gathered close in the interim.
–Larry Woiwode, "A Step From Death"

www.ingramcontent.com/pod-product-compliance
Lightning Source LLC
Chambersburg PA
CBHW051725040426
42447CB00008B/988